THE TEACHING SERMON

THE
TEACHING
SERMON

RONALD J. ALLEN

ABINGDON PRESS
Nashville

THE TEACHING SERMON

Copyright © 1995 by Abingdon Press

Library of Congress Cataloging-in-Publication Data

Allen, Ronald J. (Ronald James), 1949–
    The teaching sermon / Ronald J. Allen.
        p.   cm.
    Includes bibliographical references and index.
    ISBN 0-687-37522-3 (pbk.: alk paper)
    1. Preaching.   2. Teaching sermons.   I. Title.
BV4235.T43A44   1996
251—dc20   95-16963

95 96 97 98 99 00 01 02 03 04 — 10 9 8 7 6 5 4 3 2 1

MANUFACTURED IN THE UNITED STATES OF AMERICA

For Barek, last born son,
whose name means *blessing*,
in the hope that his life
will manifest the divine will
for each and all
to know the fullness
of life

CONTENTS

INTRODUCTION

Late one spring, the time had come to mow the yard for the first time. I pulled the mower out of storage, checked the oil, and filled it with gas. I pulled the starter cord. Nothing. I pulled again. Nothing. I pulled and pulled and pulled. Nothing. I pulled again. Surely it will start this time. No.

A crowd of neighborhood children gathered. Some of them reminded me that, as hobbies, their fathers build computers in their basements.

Persistence, I said, wins over skill. The sweat from my effort put our driveway under a flash-flood alert. Powerless, defeated, and angry, I slammed the mower into the station wagon and took it to the repair shop.

The mechanic asked, "Did you fill it with gas?" With that question, I felt a surge of emotional energy which suggested that I was the world heavyweight champion and the mechanic a practice bag.

"Well, then," the mechanic said, "did you open this?" His overalls crinkled as he reached down and turned a little valve in the fuel line that leads from the gasoline tank to the motor.

I had forgotten about that valve. But I will never forget it again, even if I live until the year 3,000. A learning event took place. The mechanic was my teacher.[1]

That experience is an analogy for me of the situation in many contemporary churches. Much is in place for the church to be a community of vital faith and life. We serve a great, living God. The Bible reveals the divine presence, promises, purposes, and power. We have a powerful tradition that can provide continuity and identity in an age of chaos and confusion, but it also can be adapted and corrected in the light of new contexts and challenges. Most of our congregations and denominations still have enough members for at least two or three to gather for worship, study, and witness. And a mission field is waiting at the edge of the church parking lot.

But many leaders, especially clergy, feel an ache in our shoulders. The gas is in the tank. The motor is ready. The need is great. We pull the starter again and again. But nothing happens.

I overstate, of course, to say that nothing happens. The doors stay open. People come. Committees meet. (In fact, some congregations functionally judge Christian maturity by the degree of their members' involvement in committee work). Pastors call in the hospitals and nursing homes, fret over major issues, and put in long days and long nights. Money goes to One Great Hour of Sharing. We work up a sweat. But the church (congregation, middle judicatory, denominational structure) seldom achieves peak performance. The engine needs more gas.

Figuratively speaking, the church needs to open the valve that connects the fuel supply to the motor. In a previous book, *The Teaching Minister,* my colleague Clark Williamson and I join a growing body of interpreters to contend that teaching the Christian faith is a primary way to get fuel from the church's tank to its theological motor.[2] We recall the utter centrality of the teaching office in Judaism and Christianity. We pose a method to help the church think theologically in ways that are adequate to the Christian vision, to the worldview of our era, and to the moral urgencies that beset us on every side. We call for pastors to be cognizant that everything in the life of the church can be an opportunity for teaching. Indeed, teaching and learning are not simply one ecclesial activity alongside others, but are constitutive of the identity of the pastor and the church. To be a pastor for a congregation is to teach.

This work explores ways in which the sermon can be a conscientious, vital part of the church's ministry of learning and teaching. The sermon is not the only educational mode in the church, but it can play a key role, for the hour of worship is the largest, most visible regular event in the community of faith. The preached word takes its place with the embodied words of baptism, the Lord's Supper, and other ministries of the church, to help express and form the congregation's vision of God, the world, and our faithful response to the presence of God in the world. The sermon can pull a starter cord that sets the gospel resonating in the consciousness of the community.

I do not want to claim too much for the teaching and learning possibilities of the sermon. Preaching, after all, is only part of the interwoven system of congregational life; all parts affect all other parts. But I suspect that many clergy take teaching for granted. Teaching can be transformative. When Annie Sullivan pressed w-a-t-e-r into the trembling hand of Helen Keller, the event disclosed hitherto unimagined possibilities in the child's world. A similar thing can happen when the preacher presses the trembling hands, hearts, and minds of the community of faith.

Of course, a sermon can do much more than teach. It can evangelize. Its prophetic cry can bring the congregation to its knees in repentance. It can render pastoral care. It can rally the congregation to protest on the town square or recruit sponsors for the youth group. It can be sacramental, mediating the knowledge of grace to the community. The number of possibilities for the function of a sermon is limited only by the number of occasions in a congregation's life. But whatever else it does, each sermon teaches something.

I do not propose a packaged formula for the teaching sermon. Learning and teaching are much too varied in purpose, occasion, content, and style of learners and teachers to be reduced to a single formula. Instead, I probe ways of thinking about teaching and learning which a creative pastor can adapt to the needs of particular texts, needs, occasions, or purposes. I offer some models of sermons that can have a teaching character; these are not exhaustive, but are intended only to help spark a preacher's imagination for teaching.

Toward this end, this book has two aims. One is to reconnoiter the ways specific sermons can have teaching and learning as their fundamental purpose. The other is to help pastors reflect on the teaching and learning possibilities inherent in each sermon and consider ways to integrate these possibilities into their regular preaching.

The first chapter outlines factors that call for a renewed focus on the teaching and learning dimensions of the sermon. The second addresses the fundamental questions, What is teaching? and How do sermons teach? The third chapter enumerates strategies that enhance learning. The fourth lays out a plan for preparing a sermon that has a teaching character. Chapter 5 describes five models for sermons that have teaching dimensions and illustrates this with abbreviated sermons. The sixth chapter contains plans for systematic teaching from the pulpit. Chapter 7 identifies crucial themes for Christian teaching today.

This approach calls for pastors who are themselves constant learners. But as every good teacher knows, the best way to learn is to prepare to teach.

I wish to express appreciation to my colleagues (and friends) at Christian Theological Seminary, Nelle G. Slater and D. Bruce Roberts, who alerted me to several pieces of literature and to concepts that would have escaped my naive eye. Arthur G. Vermillion gave a critical reading to early materials and offered a number of ideas and images that appear here. I have tried out these chapters at several conferences of clergy, and all were instructive, especially Ruth Fletcher's contribution to the Turner Lectures at Yakima, Washington. And love compels me to sigh with appreciation for my long-suffering spouse and children, who were not ready for this book to begin when the computer had hardly cooled from an earlier one.[3] The person to whom this book is dedicated reminds me daily that, of all husbands and fathers, I am most blessed.

C H A P T E R · 1

The Call to the Teaching Ministry Today

Suppose that you were interviewing with a committee from a congregation that is considering calling you as pastor. One of the members asks, "Can you give us a single word or phrase that sums up your understanding of the central work of the minister?" What would you say?

A single word or phrase can never do justice to the fullness of the ministerial calling, of course. But your response probably would reveal much about whom you understand yourself to be and what you understand yourself to be called to do. The expression you select would go a long way toward indicating what you value and do not value, how you prioritize your time, how much energy you give to (or withhold from) certain tasks.

For the past several years, I have asked this question in groups of clergy and students. The answers run a gamut through therapist, enabler, prophet, impresario, servant, change agent, wounded healer, politicial activist, priest, manager, representative. Recently, a movement has rediscovered a historic image of the clergy that is crucial for our time: the minister as teacher.

This chapter identifies three factors that call for a turn to teaching in church, in ministry, and in the sermon. First, teaching is a part of the church's identity. Second, teaching addresses an immediate (and profound) need in many contemporary churches—theological malaise. Third, teaching sermons speak to many people today.

Teaching Is Central to the Identity of Preacher and Church

In the Bible, God is the great teacher. God reveals the divine will to bless the world, as well as those things in humankind and nature that both facilitate and frustrate blessing. Thus, the psalmist prays, "Make me to know your ways, O LORD; teach me your paths" (25:4).

The Deuteronomists speak for the importance of teaching and learning in Israel. Moses reminds the people that God has charged him to teach the people the commandments, statutes, and ordinances, so that it may go well with them as they enter the Promised Land (Deut. 6:1-3):

> Keep these words that I am commanding you today in your heart. Recite them to your children and talk about them when you are at home and when you are away, when you lie down and when you rise. Bind them as a sign on your hand, fix them as an emblem on your forehead, and write them on the doorposts of your house and on your gates. (Deut. 6:6-9)

Teaching and learning which permeate everyday existence are the only adequate safeguards against idolatry.

The family is an important teaching center. Israel also developed other systems of education, so that its members would have a deep and abiding sense of God's presence and of their own identity.[1] A careful reading of the work of the priests, the prophets, and the sages reveals that teaching comprised an important part of their portfolios.[2]

The literature from the early church throbs with a similar concern.[3] The four Gospels portray Jesus as a teacher. In fact, the word *disciple* means learner. In the synoptic Gospels, Jesus' teaching interprets the dawning of the rule or kingdom of God. In the Fourth Gospel, his teaching helps the community recognize God's love for the world. In the early church, the four Gospels themselves were intended to function as teaching documents.

Teaching was among the first offices set aside by the church (e.g., I Cor. 12:27-31; Rom. 12:6-8). Teachers apparently prepared candidates for baptism and helped the established communities learn the Christian tradition, figuring out how to apply the tradition to the changing circumstances in which they found themselves. The book of Ephesians summarizes the work of the leadership in the earliest Christian communities: "Some would be . . . pastors and teachers, to equip the saints for the work of ministry, for building up the body of Christ, until all of us come to the unity of the faith and of the knowledge of the Son of God, to maturity, to the measure of the full stature of Christ" (4:11a,c, 12-13).

The church quickly drew upon the Hellenistic notion of *paideia* as a model for its life.[4] More than transferring skills and information, *paideia* formed the character of students and teachers. *Paideia* strove to enculturate a habit of thinking about the world in light of the community's deepest values and traditions, which would allow the learner to perceive and act for the good of all in any situation. The church baptized *paideia*.[5] For Clement of Alexandria and subsequent generations, "Christianity *is* paideia, divinely given in Jesus Christ and inspired Christian scriptures, focused in a profound conversion of soul, and divinely assisted by the Holy Spirit."[6] This model was influential in the church through the eighteenth century and is returning today.

In *paideia*, the teacher is not a guru, but rather a midwife, who prepares an environment in which a student's relationship to God can come to live birth.[7] This environment includes the Bible and other necessary texts, reflection upon them, and other opportunities to partake of the Christian life and practice. But God, through the Holy Spirit, ultimately brings the learner to conversion and growth.

Teaching became a part of the *raison d'etre* of the Western church. A magesterium emerged in Roman Catholicism to provide authoritative teaching and guidance, especially in the face of doctrinal controversy or changing circumstances. Teaching became an essential part of the work of bishops and priests, with the Bishop of Rome gradually becoming the major teacher of the church.[8] In the magesterial approach, teaching authority is lodged in a few individuals or bodies who speak for the whole church. Protestants (and Catholics) often note abuses within this system. But it is repeatedly able to adjust to changing times and incorporate both contemporary and past data (e.g., from philosophy and ecclesiastical tradition) into its theological reflection, with a facility that sometimes eludes Protestants.

The controversy between the Reformers and the Roman Catholic Church focused, in no small part, upon the nature of the church's teaching ministry.[9] The Reformers called for authoritative teaching from its ministers that was less hierarchical and more communitarian than that of the Roman Catholic magesterium. The Bible was nearly always an important part of Roman theological reflection, but it became primary (though not exclusive) in the Reformation theological method.

For Luther, Calvin, and their descendants, the gospel itself (as that is sometimes distinct from the Bible) is the highest authority in the church. Preaching was one of the crucial modes of teaching in all wings of the Reformation; teaching is preeminent in the homiletics of Luther: "First of all, a good preacher must be able to teach correctly and in an orderly manner."[10] The preacher is to teach Christ and nothing else. "Through the Christ of the gospels God is made known and in that life God stands at our side and comes to our aid."[11]

Calvin made the most forceful Reformation connection between preaching and teaching. For Calvin, the church is a school. God has appointed ministers to teach the congregation.[12] This is particularly true of preaching. "When Calvin is talking about preaching, the word that meets us at every turn is 'teaching'; indeed, this is very often used as a synonym for 'preaching.'" And what is taught? Regardless of biblical text or particular context, Calvin nearly always comes to this: The hidden God's self-revelation for the immediate and eternal human good, and for the human being's "grateful acceptance and submission."[13]

These emphases are characteristic of nearly all the churches that trace their origins directly or indirectly to the Reformation.[14] Who are we? Communities that teach, learn, and witness to the gospel.

The Contemporary Church Is in a Theological Malaise

The malaise of the contemporary church adds a voice to the call for the teaching ministry. The statistics of the institutional decline (loss of members, loss of financial muscle, loss of influence in the larger culture) of the long-established churches are so well known that they need no repetition here.[15] These trends may intensify as the long-established denominations become increasingly geriatric.

How did this situation come about? It is widely believed that the long-established denominations are losing members in droves to strict and conservative churches. This is a myopic opinion. Statistical studies show that every member who migrates to a strict or conservative congregation is replaced by one who migrates back.[16]

The institutional decline of the long-established churches results from a complex of determinants that include low birth rates, large numbers of congregations located in parts of the country where the population is not growing, very few new congregations being started, honest membership rolls, lethargic membership recruitment, and ineffective programming.

Larger factors are also at work. A major cultural shift is taking place across the United States.[17] Prior to the 1960s, virtually everyone (at least on a popular level) was Protestant, Roman Catholic, or Jewish. In addition to the meaning that affiliation with church or synagogue could bring to a human life, it was socially advantageous to be a part of the church. Church membership rolls benefited from this perception.

However, the Christian community no longer enjoys a favored cultural status. Two buzzwords describe the new reality: pluralism and diversity. Religious affiliation is no longer socially expected. In a diverse pluralistic society, religious (and nonreligious) options compete with one another in the marketplace of human loyalties.

The pluralism of our day can hasten the time when the whole human family can live in shalom. The many elements in the human family might learn to come together. Such a reunion depends upon whether the diverse communities can develop mutual respect and concern, in the midst of differences over race, ethnicity, politics, economics, gender, and religion. However, in the midst of diversity and its relativities, the long-established churches have not articulated a clear vision that energizes significant numbers of members or that proves inviting to outsiders.

Most of the people who disappear from the long-established denominations disappear from religion altogether. "The big 'winner' in the switching game is the growing secular constituency."[18] Since 1952, the number of persons who are unaffiliated with religion has increased by 350 percent. Most of those who disaffiliate are young (under the age of 45), well educated, oriented to personal growth, and interested in alternative lifestyles.[19]

Why do they leave the church? They do not find the message and life of the church significant enough to justify their thought, loyalty, time, and money. The basic purpose of religion is to help the community make sense of life from the perspective of ultimate reality. Evidently, the disaffiliated feel that they get as much meaning for life from Rotary, *The New Republic*, The American Association of University Women, *Psychology Today*, the Sierra Club, and jogging, as from the church.

This coheres with other data. The Lilly Endowment funded major investigations of several long-established denominations. The study of my denomination is representative. Its director, D. Newell Williams, concludes that the Christian Church (Disciples of Christ) suffers from theological amnesia. This community does not have a *distinctive* Christian norm for making sense of the church, its message and mission, or the larger culture.[20] Why should I become a part of the church, if I can feel that I get the same life benefits from other activities that ask so much less of me?

Similarly, in the late 1980s, a research body called The Search Institute analyzed the level of faith maturity in the church, as well as factors that encourage faith to deepen. The researchers interviewed more than 11,000 church members and probed more than 560 congregations in the historic denominations. The study determined: "Only a minority of Protestant adults evidence the kind of integrated, vibrant and life-encompassing faith that congregations seek to develop. For most adults, faith is underdeveloped, lacking some of the key elements necessary to maturity."[21]

While pastors often lament the biblical illiteracy of our congregations, this study intimates a more penetrating difficulty: widespread theological illiteracy. To be sure, the church is not alone. The church's theological illiteracy is part of a growing cultural illiteracy.[22] But that is small comfort, for many Christians do not have a clear vision of the church's message, its sources of authority, or how to come to informed theological judgments about matters of belief and behavior. On the bright side, the study found that participation in Christian education is the most important stimulation to mature faith. This commends a reemphasis on teaching and learning in the church.

Contemporary Preaching Shares Complicity in This Theological Illiteracy

An empirical investigation of more than 200 sermons preached in the Christian Church (Disciples of Christ) finds that the preachers do not wrestle in a significant way with "the complexity and moral ambiguity of the daily life struggles faced by the congregation." The sermons speak in language that "is almost completely abstract rather than specific." Further, "The assumption would appear to be that the congregation knows and understands the doctrine and thus needs simply to be reassured that God does indeed love us, will forgive us, and save us. But it is clearly dangerous to assume much doctrinal sophistication or even Biblical literacy on the part of a congregation."[23]

The church thus has a profound need for reinvigoration of teaching and learning. The pastor is a primary figure in this recovery. However, a wild card is in the deck. After surveying changes in preaching among northern Presbyterians during the last several decades, John McClure concludes, "What seems to be missing in Presbyterian preaching now . . . is a consistent and assertive theological message." McClure finds, further, that there are often "inconsistencies and even counteracting theological messages at work from one sermon to another."[24] Teaching and learning sometimes need to begin with remedial work in the pastor's study, to articulate a coherent theological vision.[25]

The preacher must provide a distinctive statement of transcendent reality, through which the church can make sense of itself and of the world. The sermon must articulate a coherent vision of the gospel that offers good news to the listeners and provides norms by which to measure all that the church says and does, in order to evaluate the larger world and its own life. In the midst of pluralism and relativism, the sermon should give the church a place to stand that is firmly grounded, yet open to fresh insight and discovery.

Further, the church is rediscovering that all of its phases have teaching and learning potential. The church is a life system in which each part affects and is affected by the other parts.[26] Christian education takes place not simply in the activities sponsored by the Christian Education Committee, but throughout community life. In the broad sense, all that takes place in a congregation teaches, for everything communicates what is of God and what is not, what is true or false, what is important and unimportant, what is approved and disapproved.[27] Therefore, a simple question should be asked of each moment of the congregation's life: What is the church actually teaching here? Is it enacting the Christian vision, or something else?

While participation in Christian education events is a most important doorway to faith development, Search Institute found that five additional qualities in a congregation also enhance growth toward Christian maturity: a climate of warmth and acceptance; care received, particularly through small groups; opportunities for service to others; a thinking climate; and uplifting worship.[28]

In this book, I am most interested in preaching as a teaching event. Of course, the service of worship is not primarily educational. Worship first honors God and provides opportunities for the community to speak with God and to receive signs of God's presence and providence. But through the liturgy, the congregation learns what is true of God and what is not, what God offers and asks, how the community can appropriately (or inappropriately) respond to God and to one another. For instance, a hymn that praises God as "pure, unbounded love" both speaks to God and teaches the congregation that God's love is without limit.[29]

The sermon is a key teaching moment. The service of worship is the largest regular gathering of the congregation. The preacher thus has a remarkable opportunity to invite people to grow in faith.

Teaching Sermons Appeal to Many People Today

Even if a pastor is not yet persuaded that teaching the Christian vision will counter the current theological malaise, other qualities intimate that our time is right for sermons with teaching and learning characteristics. As the title of one of his books reveals, Wade Clark Roof finds that the baby boomers are *A Generation of Seekers*. To be sure, in their youth and young adulthood, a larger percentage of this generation dropped out of organized religion than had previous generations. But in their middle years, they yearn for a way of being in the world that can help them see, feel, and act in a unified, purposeful manner.

The new values emphasize self-fulfillment and self-growth, inner spiritual discovery and exploration. A greater sense of self, appreciation of the body, of gender and spirituality, of reaching out to others, and of letting go are all themes that find common expression.

Boomers are growing older, and many are approaching midlife and a phase of reflection that encourages greater clarity of who they are and a more balanced sense of commitment in their lives. Older boomers especially—inside and outside organized religion, both liberals and conservatives—are spiritually sensitive and seeking answers to the perennial questions about the meaning and purpose of life.[30]

Their spiritual quest takes them to places ranging from Eastern religions to self-help programs, to conservative Christianity, to the solitude of their own contemplations. But boomers share a common substructure. They want to make sense of life.

The boomers distinguish institutional religion from the quest for meaning. They are not as much interested in formally affiliating with an established church as in understanding their existence. The church that appeals to them has vital programs for children and opportunities for adult growth in a context of clear thinking, respect for freedom of thought, feeling, belonging, and concern for others. Congregations that falter at these basic tasks will not catch their attention.[31]

Preaching that helps the listeners to find meaningful links between their experiences and the Christian vision (which, indeed, offers a unified way of thinking, feeling, and acting) can speak to this generation. Roof's research focused on the baby boomers. But his emphasis on the search for a meaningful framework within which to understand existence is central to other generations as well. Many in North America are searching.[32]

In a time of spiritual quest, a sermon with qualities of teaching and learning appeals to many people as it brings together quest and Christian tradition. Lyle Schaller notices the following characteristics about churches in which the congregation understands the sermon as a teaching event: the average attendance is higher than in the typical congregation of the long-established denominations; the average age is much younger; the congregation tends to be growing in size; attenders believe that they are deepening in faith.[33] Schaller finds further that sermons are particularly attractive when they are explicitly designed for people on a religious pilgrimage. Searchers frequently respond, "I want to come back and hear more." Happily, established members find such sermons "enlightening, meaningful, and affirming."[34]

The most obvious examples of the attractiveness of teaching sermons, perhaps, are the burgeoning congregations in which the sermon is a running commentary on a passage from scripture. The preacher explains the text, often verse by verse, and relates it to the community.

I pause over this argument (teaching sermons have appeal) and this example (the sermon as running commentary) to respond to four thoughtful reservations which I frequently hear from pastors in the established denominations:

1. Some pastors rightly point out that faithfulness to the gospel, not statistical measure, is the ultimate criterion for evaluating the success of the sermon and the life of the church. They reason that there is no necessary correlation between faithfulness and popular appeal. In fact, some congregations that call themselves Christian seem to thrive on sermons (and faith) that have minimal relationship to historic Christian tradition. Other congregations appear to have faithful preaching of the gospel, but languish in institutional health. Nonetheless, there is no reason to *assume* that popular attraction and unfaithfulness always go together. Today, as in the first century C.E., the preaching of the gospel can attract large numbers of people.

2. Some pastors sometimes resist the idea of teaching sermons because they think of teaching sermons only in the genre of running commentary. They claim this is too limiting. I respond: quite right. There is no single formula or genre to define the teaching sermon. Teaching sermons can take as many forms as there are pastors.

By way of parenthesis, I add that verse-by-verse preaching is frequently welcomed in long-established congregations. James Fish, an administrator at Wartburg Theological Seminary, reports that his sermons worked through texts verse by verse in several congregations. In comparison to other styles of preaching, "These 'expository Bible studies' have drawn the strongest positive response from the congregations."[35] Many pastors shift to this kind of preaching at their mid-week service, or employ it in a mid-week adult Bible study. I believe this style of preaching needs to be recovered in the long-established congregations as a part of a pastor's inventory of homiletical approaches.

3. Pastors sometimes vehemently raise a theological objection to sermons in the style of running commentary. These sermons are frequently associated with theological positions distasteful to pastors trained in critical theological thinking. This reservation is reinforced by the fact that some of the most well-known teaching preachers are found on television. The histrionics of the electronic church embarrass many clergy.

I reply that we need not throw out the baby with the bath water. Clergy in the long-established churches do not need to compromise theological content in order to teach.[36] Histrionics are not required for a teaching pulpit. A teaching emphasis in the pulpit can be in a style that is congenial to the community's theology.

4. Pastors often point out that congregational growth (both numerically and in faith maturity) is usually the result of multiple factors, not just attractive preaching. This is correct. Theology, a wide variety of options offered in congregational life, aggressiveness of recruiting, the location of the building, the entrepreneurial personality of the pastor—all these (and more) contribute to statistical evidences of health. However, teaching sermons are often a part of the equation in congregations that are growing.

Teaching sermons are one way for people feel that the sermon is participating in the most important function of religion: to make sense of life in the light of transcendent reality.[37] Teaching sermons respond to this need. Skillful teaching preachers can even encourage listeners to become aware of needs that listeners had not recognized.

When the sermon vitally interprets God and life, the congregation comes alive as a listening community. The typical preaching textbook recommends that a sermon last no more than twenty minutes (or even fifteen or twelve) because the attention span of today's listener has been truncated by exposure to the electronic media. The latter, it is said, pattern the consciousness of the listener to short, fast moving, highly sensory bites. The media create images which bypass critical thought and impress themselves on the sensorium of the receiver. We are told that today's listeners have difficulty following arguments.

However, in congregations in which the teaching sermon is the norm, the sermon can be as long as twenty-five, thirty, or forty minutes.[38] The sermons contain ideas, analysis, argument, historical recollection, and doctrinal exposition, as well as story and metaphor. The congregation appears to be willing to work at listening.

How can we account for this? At the simplest level, some congregations are socialized to sit through a long sermon. This suggests that many congregations could be socialized toward longer attention spans.

Further, good teaching preachers are good communicators. They speak with energy, clarity, conviction, colorful speech, pathos, humor, practicality. They vivify ideas and stories. Listeners identify with the message. The congregation feels as if it is participating in the sermon.[39] The best teaching preachers make critical use of aspects of media-shaped communication strategies. But these sermons are not "made for TV."[40] They have theological substance, critical reflection, emotive power, and moral drive. They honor the integrity and freedom of the listeners.

Of course, preachers can use communication techniques also for manipulation and falsehood. But at their best, a communicative teacher leads the congregation into a sermon in which the congregation engages the gospel and the world in an active, critical way.

When the preacher is a lively communicator and the content of the sermon makes an important existential connection, the congregation is all ears (and for prolonged periods of time). Peter Gomes, pastor of the Harvard Memorial Church, whose sermons often have a teaching slant, normally preaches thirty-five to forty minutes to rapt congregations. I have seldom heard Fred Craddock, whose preaching often has an inductive teaching objective, speak for less than thirty minutes, even in congregations that are accustomed to fifteen-minute sermons. Gomes and Craddock are unusually gifted preachers, but their repeated capacity to sustain interest is rooted less in homiletical technique than in the fact that they bring life experience into the presence of the gospel, so that listeners understand themselves and the world from the standpoint of ultimate reality.

I do not lobby for longer sermons. A boring sermon that does not connect God and life is too long if it lasts only twelve minutes. But people's willingness to sit through (and return again and again for) lengthy sermons shows that the vital teaching of the gospel can penetrate even the restless, illiterate, non-reading MTV mind and heart.

The time is ripe for the preacher to develop an image of the sermon as a teaching event. We turn now to the next questions. What is teaching in the Christian community? and How can sermons become opportunities for learning and teaching?

C H A P T E R • 2

What Is a
Teaching Sermon?

The preacher steps to the pulpit, mouth slightly dry, a little nervous. In the pastor's Thursday evening Bible study group, it had become embarrassingly clear that the congregation has only a caricature notion of one of the denomination's cherished beliefs. This morning, the pastor expects to preach a teaching sermon to help enlarge the congregation's understanding. So as not to assault the congregation from a bully pulpit, the preacher needs to have a clear understanding of teaching in the Christian community. The preacher needs to discover ways in which all sermons teach. And in order to meet expectations, the preacher should know the characteristics of sermons that are specifically intended to be teaching sermons.

Teaching in the Christian Community

At its heart, Christian teaching is helping the community name the world (and its experience in the world) in terms of the gospel.[1] By *experience*, I mean the fullness of all that happens to the congregation and to its members.[2] The gospel is the news of God's unconditional love for each and every created entity, and God's unfailing will for justice for each and every creature. Thus, the calling of Christian teaching is to encourage the congregation to recognize how the presence of God (particularly God's faithful love for all and God's unremitting will for justice for all) affects every moment of life. As Richard R. Osmer puts it, a teaching church helps the congregation discern "a normative vision of the

Christian life and invites people to discover what their real needs are as they seek to live out this vision."[3]

The Christian teacher is a helper or guide in the learning process. A teacher cannot force learning. But a Christian teacher can hope to create an environment or activity in which the learning community can obtain a clear angle of vision on the subject matter, explore it, come to discovery, evaluate the discovery in a critical way according to norms of Christian faith, make a conscious decision to own (or not to own) the discovery, and design a plan (if needed) to implement the discovery. The teacher helps the students discern criteria for choosing among alternatives of interpretation and to think critically about the issue or situation. The whole process of learning may not take place in each singular event, but over time, a good teacher guides students into complete critical thinking about Christian faith.

According to Northrop Frye, a teacher is "someone who attempts to re-create the subject in the students' minds." The teacher first tries to have the students identify what they potentially already know. Teaching "includes breaking up the power of repression" in the minds of the students which prevents them from acknowledging what they know.[4] It also includes providing access to additional material necessary for the students' growth.[5]

Christian teaching hopes to affect the gestalt, the whole being and becoming of the learner.[6] It seeks to touch mind, feelings, behavior, and their interaction. Christian learning may confirm. It may intensify. It may result in reexamination. It may call for change, large or small. In a specific situation of learning and teaching, the focus may be more on one aspect than on another; teaching may focus more on the mind than on the heart or will, or it may focus on the heart more than on the will or mind. But a perceptive Christian teacher knows that thought, heart, and will are so conjoined that when one is moved, all are moved. The whole self is affected.

The teacher tries to create situations that seem most promising to help students mature. These experiences can vary. Subject matters differ in their requirements, as do styles of learning. For instance, one group of students may most need basic information to help them navigate Christian terrain, while others may need to explore the hidden recesses of their inner lives in potentially painful or explosive ways, while still others may need to learn how to mobilize for community action. The teacher may be information giver, question asker, mentor, gadfly, guide, mediator, antiexample, poet. The teacher may need to withhold information or speak in paradox, to help the lesson distill in the students' minds.[7] The teacher's specific role should fit both subject matter and students.

However, a Christian teacher is not just a cafeteria manager who passes options before the learners. The Christian teacher aims not only to expose students to alternative points of view, but to help the congregation weigh those alternatives carefully. In the church, the teacher is often an advocate for a specific position. Indeed, the Christian teacher is not just one of the guys and gals in the learning circle. The church sets the teacher apart to represent Christianity in the learning situation. But Christian teaching should honor the freedom of the student to say No, even when No is a mistake.

Christian teaching involves two pivotal moments. The first is *remembering* (or *becoming acquainted with*) the content of the Christian tradition. If today's church is to make sense of its own tradition, it first must know what is in that tradition. This tradition is in the Bible and in the verbal and nonverbal phenomena of the church, from the biblical era into the present. Ordinarily, a learning event in the Christian community ought to help the congregation bring the tradition specifically to mind. The congregation occasionally may be able to remember pertinent elements of the tradition, but frequently, the people will need to learn about these elements from scratch.[8] For, as we noted in the previous chapter, our church is theologically illiterate. The teacher cannot casually refer to the story of Jacob or the missionary journeys of Paul or Augustine's view of sin. These need to be spelled out. In this respect, Christian teaching seeks to create a community of theological memory.[9] Two caveats are in order:

1. "The" Christian tradition is not a monolith. It contains many different nuances. Of course, many elements are common to nearly all Christian communities. Virtually all Christians believe in a God of gracious love who is revealed through Jesus Christ. Nearly all believe that sin has radically warped God's purposes for the world and that God is working to redeem the world. Nonetheless, particular Christian denominations, groups, or thinkers develop their own nuances of emphasis. The Christian teacher needs to respect

these differences, even while arguing for a normative point of view.

2. Seldom can a teacher deal with the whole of the Christian tradition on a single occasion. Normally, teachers ask the community to remember or learn about a selected aspect of the tradition (for example, a passage from the Bible or a significant event—such as baptism). But in so doing, teachers need to help the congregation discern how the piece fits into the whole. When congregations begin to mistake an individual piece of tradition for the whole, idolatry can easily follow.

The second pivotal moment is *interpreting* the significance of the tradition for the learning community in its contemporary setting. The tradition is not simply a commodity that can be passed on from one setting or generation to another. The tradition is alive. Some things are being added to it, while others are dropping out.

In Mary Elizabeth Moore's memorable picture, the tradition reaches us much like Noah's Ark.[10] It is filled with animals. Some are obviously helpful. Some are very strange and we don't know quite what to do with them. Others appear dangerous. The Christian teacher helps the congregation classify the animals on the ark of Christian tradition and figure out how to relate to them.

To put it more formally, Christian teaching leads the community to reflect critically upon the tradition and its relationship to the contemporary church and world. How does the tradition directly inform the community? What points seem odd, even insignificant, but may become instructive when viewed from a different perception? Have some voices been lost but now need to be heard afresh? What contributions, past and contemporary, might be added to the tradition to strengthen its witness? What aspects of the tradition are invidious and need to be challenged, corrected, or dropped? The Christian teacher encourages the community to recognize lines of continuity and change in its relationship with the tradition. And in the process, the tradition itself is transformed. Christian teaching helps the community take its own place in the unfolding of the tradition. Some theologians speak of this process as *tradition-ing*.[11]

The goal of Christian teaching and learning is not to interpret the tradition for its own sake. *The goal is to help the church become aware of, and responsive to, the gracious presence and purposes of the living God as revealed through Jesus Christ*. The Christian teacher hopes to lead the community into consciousness of the divine presence and to guide the community in responding to the fullness of that presence with fullness of discipleship.

Charles R. Blaisdell points out that Christian teaching often has a dual focus—deconstructive and constructive. It should expose the falsehoods, relativities, and idols that human beings treat as true, ultimate, and transcendent: "The minister-as-teacher is the one who discerns and creates a world that is centered on the ultimacy of God; he or she aptly and appropriately names idolatries and calls them into question from this transcendent perspective."[12] In this respect, teaching may have a disturbing quality, both to the learners and to the teachers. "It tests and questions people. It elicits responses from them that alter perceptions, change courses of action, and require hard decisions. Teachers confront people with their finitude. They point to their mandate. They identify the source of their security and they question their idolatries."[13]

But Christian teaching is *primarily* constructive: "Veracious preaching constructs or discerns an alternative to the idolatries present before the preacher. As such, preaching is, or can be, redemptive, hope-evoking, and energizing."[14] Preaching can have these latter qualities, as Thomas Oden says, when it is rooted in "an intense awareness of the holy in the midst of our concrete life revealed through human speech."[15]

To this point, I have focused on Christian teaching as helping the congregation recognize, critically internalize, and behave according to the content of the Christian tradition. I focus on content because the primary need of the contemporary church is at that point. *We most need a revitalized apprehension of the reality of God.* Our recent anemia results less from ineffective method than from inadequate vision.

But the question of method comes up. Some leaders in Christian education think it axiomatic that good learning events must be participatory. The students must actively do something—for example, talk or expressive themselves artistically. The sermon, then, would be a poor approach to learning, because the congregation appears to be passive. Mary Boys summarizes research which undercuts this conclusion:

Many "progressive" educators have presumed that the warmth of the teacher's personality, a democratic system of classroom management, and an increase in pupil talk are superior to a situation in which the teacher is more directive (these are the broad categories measured by the Flanders System of Interaction Analysis), but the evidence does not support such a presupposition. Similarly, many presume that lecturing is a poor mode of teaching and that discussion is better. Again, the evidence does not substantiate this.[16]

Many models can effectively lead to learning, if the models are well handled, if they fit particular learning situations, and if they provide learners with access to the materials necessary for growth. A sermon can bring a subject to life for a congregation.

John McClure points out that a good preacher can shape the monological presentation so that it has a dialogical character.[17] The speaker helps the listeners find themselves in the presentation: their stories, their struggles, their hopes. They may not speak aloud during the sermon, but they are not passive receivers. They very much participate in the unfolding of the sermon or lecture.[18]

Of course, the sermon has limitations as a learning event. The preacher may not have enough time for a sufficient treatment of the subject. The sermon may spark moments of insight that cry for immediate conversation. It may raise questions that turn the soul inside out. It may generate intense feelings that need attention before the listeners can return to the flow of the sermon.

Every mode of learning has its limitations. Sensitive preachers and congregations can become communities of support for those touched by the sermon. The best situation may be one in which the congregation has the opportunity to respond directly to the sermon with questions, comments, and dialogue. Toward this end, some congregations organize groups that respond to the sermon after the service. But even without feedback, a sermon can be a genuine help to a congregation's learning.[19]

All Sermons Teach

Given this understanding of teaching, it is obvious that all sermons have teaching dimensions. The preacher may not design every sermon to be a learning event, but each sermon has the effect of helping the congregation name the world in terms of the gospel.

A sermon typically has one of two broad purposes. It is directed either to persons who have never made a confession of faith or to a congregation of believers.[20] In a general sense, the purpose of the first is to evangelize the unconverted, while the second is to build up the established church.

The long-established denominations do not have a conscious strategy for evangelism today. Much of what we call evangelism is not so much carrying the gospel to persons who have never heard it (or who have turned away from it) but is more a form of membership recruitment. We offer membership to visitors to our congregations (and this is not quite what seekers are seeking). Preachers in the established denominations do not often have opportunities from the pulpit to discuss the Christian faith with persons who do not already believe. The historic churches need to formulate an evangelistic witness.[21] What strategies can we use to speak the gospel (either through direct spoken word or through media) so that it has a chance to be received by those who do not know it?

Even now, however, without altering their Sunday sermons, preachers in established communities have occasional opportunities to interest some nonbelievers or would-be believers or partial believers. Fred Craddock recalls earlier years when congregations invited guest preachers for evangelistic meetings. The evangelist targeted the unconverted, but the sermon was overheard by church members who, "out of the line of fire" and relaxed by "freedom, anonymity, and distance" were stirred by the "breeze passing overhead." "If sermons to the unconverted are heard effectively by those believers present who really overhear them, would it not be reasonable to assume that sermons addressed to the membership might be effectively overheard by any present who are not yet disciples?" Craddock concludes, "It is not only regrettable but sinful that visitors who overhear pastors speaking to the membership quite often find themselves listening in on announcements, scoldings, and faint pep rallies."[22]

Sermons to an established congregation do teach, even when teaching is not their main purpose. For instance, during the fall, the congregation may have a campaign to raise support for its budget. Sermons during this campaign often are designed to motivate members to pledge to the budget. But in the process, the sermons signal the congregation as to what the preacher believes to be an authentic Christian understanding of money and its use. Or the state legislature may be about to vote to reinstate the death penalty. The pastor may aim for a series of sermons to galvanize the congregation to join the demonstration against the death penalty on the steps of the state capitol. These sermons help the congregation identify the extent and nature of God's unconditional love.

Sermons also teach *implicitly*, by what the preacher addresses and what the preacher does not address. The attention—or inattention—we give to a subject is often a gauge of its importance. When sermons repeatedly devote their real energy to psychotherapy and give little focus to theology, the congregation soon gets the picture that theology is standing at the guest book, but psychotherapy is the bride. Silence often implies consent. For example, in a racist society, a pulpit that seldom addresses racial matters can be heard as supporting racism.

Sermons teach implicitly too by including and ignoring different kinds of people. If sermons focus exclusively on those similar to the members of the congregation (say, middle-class Euro-Americans), the preacher implicitly teaches that these persons are most important. Sermons that mention a broad range of people suggest that God values the whole human family.

As a corollary, sermons that portray some people or situations in stereotypes or caricature implicitly teach that those stereotypes and caricatures are acceptable to the Christian vision. Sermons that discuss people and situations in honesty and complexity remind the congregation that God views people and situations in the same way, that stereotype and caricature are out of place in the Christian worldview.

Sermons also teach implicitly through their homiletical styles. A style that is open and inviting and collegial teaches that learning (and relationships) in the Christian community are the same. A sermon that is unilateral and abrasive and legalistic legitimates such patterns of learning and relationship.

Furthermore, sermons implicitly teach theological method. Preachers model their theological method on the way they think through the analysis of a life situation or a doctrine or a biblical text. Simply by listening, members pick up cues on useful (or trivial) questions, lines of approach, modes of research, hermeneutical movements.

The preacher needs to be critically conscious of the implicit curriculum of the pulpit. Is the range of the preacher's concerns sufficient for a gospel of universal, unconditional love and justice? Are sermons loving and just in their homiletical approaches?[23] Am I teaching the congregation to think theologically in the most helpful ways?

What Is a Teaching Sermon?

Beyond the fact that all sermons have teaching dimensions, some sermons are designed specifically to teach. What are the characteristics of such sermons? What are their distinguishing features? Following are some representative ways in which teaching sermons have been discussed in recent homiletical theory.

Richard A. Jensen regards the didactic sermon as one that abstracts the lessons, or points, from a biblical text. The preacher aims at the mind of the listener and develops points in a logical, sequential manner (much as one would develop written material), with the goal of leading the hearer to believe that the ideas of the sermon are true.[24]

James Cox implies that sermons which have teaching character offer explanation and argumentation.[25] John Westerhoff regards the teaching or instructional sermon as one whose purpose is to inform. The sermon contains systematic exposition of Christian concepts (such as biblical texts or Christian doctrines), logically put together.[26]

James Earl Massey takes the doctrinal sermon and the teaching sermon to be synonymous. The teaching sermon gives an explanation of the truths necessary for faith and salvation. As a result of the sermon, the believer should come to understand the relationship of these truths to personal and social experience.[27] William J. Carl also expects the teaching sermon to be focused on Christian doctrine. Its particular focus is the mind. The teaching pastor hopes to bring the congregation to "the highest possible definiteness." The teaching pastor helps the listeners to know what they believe and why they believe it, so that they can live the Christian faith.[28]

Author H. Grady Davis sees the teaching sermon as drawing out the implications of the Christian faith, so that hearers can understand the "meaning and basis" of Christian existence and grasp the Christian content, with the result that their lives conform to the Christian faith.[29]

Robert Hughes rightly calls attention to a core of information that is essential to Christian identity and functioning.[30] Information can be transformative. I remember, for instance, the first time I turned to the map in my study Bible and saw the great distance from Ur (the home of Abram and Sarah) to Palestine. That information deepened my appreciation for the risk involved in faith. It would be difficult to overestimate the value of a clear and confident answer to the question put to some Christian assertions by people hanging onto hope by their fingernails: "How do you know this is true?"[31]

If a church is to recover from its theological anemia and run in the marathon of contemporary life, it needs to understand (conceptually and existentially) its own language and doctrine. When faced with the necessity of making a prophetic statement that is immensely unpopular, the witnessing community needs to know, deep in its heart, what it believes and why. When storm winds blow against such a witness, the church needs to give an account that is more substantial than, "Our position just feels right."

Thomas Long notes that contemporary preaching (with its permeating emphasis on story and image) easily becomes "like Windham Hill music—beautiful, lilting, moody, but not the least assertive and with absolutely nothing to teach."[32] Some Christians can no longer think about their faith logically and critically. They simply emote.

Conceptual sermons which emphasize explanation and argument are a helpful corrective. The coming years need to bring many such sermons into the presence of the congregation.

Nonetheless, these notions of the teaching sermon are limited in three ways. First, they are too restricted, in that they present teaching largely as an appeal to intellectual understanding. As we noted in the first part of this chapter, Christian teaching seeks to touch the heart and will, as well as the mind. Human understanding is a gestalt. Sometimes feeling precedes cognitive grasp. Sometimes behavior becomes the occasion for reflection which leads to more precise thought and contributes to deeper feeling. One of the teacher's creative roles is to assess the best point of entry for teaching. Do we begin with mind? emotion? activity? And how do we integrate the whole?

Second, they are too restricted in their teaching and learning methods. While teaching and learning certainly can involve facts, logical reasoning, and argument, they also can involve other kinds of data and experiences. For example, Christian communities learn through participation in activities. Taking part in our congregation's rotation at a local shelter for the homeless was a learning event for our thirteen-year-old son, especially when he came face to face with a classmate from his school who was living at the shelter. "No one teaching style will suffice to convey the totality of the Christian gospel. . . . There are some aspects of the gospel that can only be taught with a hymn, a poem, or a story."[33]

Learning sometimes takes place without our being aware of it. Knowledge, feelings, desired behaviors simply become a part of our reservoir of being. In the Christian community, however, learning is at its best when it includes critical reflection, in which the community and its members evaluate what is (or is not) being taken into Christian orientation.

Third, some of these scholars restrict the teaching sermon to the doctrinal sermon. No one could agree more than I that Christian doctrine (in the sense of systematic theological exposition of Christian belief which takes account of Scripture, tradition, experience, and reason) is urgently needed in the church today.[34] Doctrine furnishes a framework within which to understand the bits and pieces of the Christian life. Whether or not the preacher is conscious of it, each sermon is preached from the standpoint of Christian doctrine. But the contemporary Christian community also needs to learn more than systematic exposition of doctrine.

The teaching sermon is distinguished not so much by its form or method but by its purpose. The primary purpose of a teaching sermon is to help the congregation name (or rename) some aspect of its world experience in terms of the gospel. The sermon is consciously designed to encourage the community to grow in some aspect of Christian awareness or action. A sermon whose primary purpose is teaching comes about when the pastor discerns that the congregation needs to enhance its gospel perception or praxis, and conscientiously designs a sermon to lead the congregation into that larger reality.[35]

For instance, the community may need to have ignorance or misinformation supplanted by correct information. The theological memory may grow faint and need to be refreshed. The people may need a deeper intuitive apprehension and attentiveness to the divine presence. Christians may be behaving contrary to Christian norms because they do not see any contradiction between norm and practice. The church may be capable of more intense joy than it has experienced thus far. The situations that call for teaching sermons are as many as the moments of life.

The teaching preacher selects a homiletical approach that seems suited to the content of what needs to be taught, to the congregation's receptiveness to the subject, and to the possibilities for growth available within the time allotted for the sermon. One teaching sermon may provide information and argument. Another may create an affective experience (with critical reflection). Still another may analyze some behavior of the congregation or of the world. The preacher thus must be a perceptive interpreter of the local listeners and be able to think creatively about how to help lead the community into an encounter that has a good chance of resulting in learning. When preaching in the teaching mode, the pastor:

- assists the congregation to have a clear view of the subject;
- sets out the importance of the subject to the Christian community;
- sets out the basic questions that are integral to understanding or experience of the subject;
- helps the community gather resources and norms that can make Christian sense of the subject;
- leads the community in critical reflection on the topic;
- places the subject in relationship with the congregation's larger worlds;
- encourages the congregation to see how Christian teaching relates to their daily thought, feeling, and practice.

The sermon may be an informational lecture. It may be an argument. It may be an extended image. It may be a political-theological analysis. But it will help the community name its experience in the world, in the terms of God's unconditional love and faithful will for justice. We turn to practical strategies for doing so in the remainder of the book.

An important presupposition underlies the idea that the preacher is a teacher in the Christian community. The preacher must be continually learning about God, the world, the church, and the sacred traditions of the Christian community. This calls for two brief observations. First, theological emptiness is not limited to laity today. All of us, as clergy, need to refuel our tanks of theological wisdom. Second, as experienced teachers know, one of the best ways to learn is to prepare to teach. Preparing the teaching sermon thus will often benefit both laity and clergy. The preacher's own freshness and depth as a student will greatly contribute to the congregation's willingness to regard the pastor as a trusted guide in the journey of faith, whom they will join on adventures of discovery.

C H A P T E R • 3

How People Learn from Sermons

The teaching preacher can incorporate into the sermon some characteristics of the ways people learn. In one sense, this is an impossible matter to explain. Educators have long studied how people learn, and one of the most important discoveries from these studies is that variables in learning differ enormously from person to person. At different stages in life, people learn in different ways.[1] People develop their own styles of learning.[2] Women and men often process information and learn differently.[3] Intelligence plays a role. Nonetheless, despite such diversity, some characteristics seem to be common to many of the best learning experiences.

Here I focus on modes of expression and experience that facilitate adult learning and can be directly helpful to the preacher.[4] Mary C. Boys waves a warning flag along this road. Even the best of the research into modes of teaching and learning cannot result in readymade recipes or foolproof techniques for teaching.[5] The preacher's own creativity and sensitivity to the congregation are the crucial factors in knowing which of these possibilities to employ and which to save for another sermon.

The Relationship Between Teacher and Learner

The relationship between the teacher and the learner is a key to learning. In the optimum learning situation, the student trusts the teacher both as a guide and as a person.[6] Positive benefits result from such a trusting relationship: the learner tends to be open to the possibilities offered by the teacher; the student has confidence in the teacher and in the way the teacher is guiding the learning community into the subject. If the students encounter difficulty in the material, they are likely to give the material more serious consideration if they trust the teacher. This last point is particularly true when the learning community finds itself dealing with ideas, values, and practices that are in tension with, even contradictions of their preexisting attitudes and practices. From the teachers' side, teachers are much more likely to give themselves fully and freely to the learning when they feel trusted.

What generates trust?[7] Teachers are most likely to be trusted by a student when they:

- are authentically themselves in the classroom, and their personality and behavior is the same in the classroom, at the water fountain, in personal conference with students, on the tennis court;
- are clearly knowledgeable about the subject under study;
- manifest congruity between their words and their actions and are honest;
- model useful interaction with the subject matter;
- treat all students equally and do not play favorites;
- listen carefully to students and take seriously student concerns and questions;
- communicate that they have empathy with the learners;
- can articulate their vision for the purpose of the event;
- give evidence of careful preparation, yet are willing to adjust plans to fit the situation;
- share their own experiences with the subject matter;
- make it clear that the students' growth (not the teachers' professional advancement or other extraneous concern) is the driving force in the teacher's presence in the learning situation;
- respect the fact that students must do their own learning, but accept their own roles as leaders and do not deny their own credibility;
- are willing to talk with students about their lives (the lives of both teacher and student) outside the classroom.

Teachers must communicate respect for the students; this is one of the most important things a teacher must do. Students' learning potentials rise exponentially when they feel that the teacher accepts them and values them as persons of worth.[8] This is decisive when the teacher is leading the students into arenas where the teacher's vision and the students' predilections differ.

Toward this end, the teacher may find it useful to say directly, "Now, I know that on this point some of us will disagree, but it is important to respect one another and try to understand viewpoints other than our own." The teacher also needs to help the students have a sense of respect for one another, particularly when they disagree.

The teacher aims to create a "safe space" in which students can encounter the subject matter without feeling so threatened that they cease interacting with the subject.[9] Students are most open to new notions when they are aware that the leader accepts them and that the learning community will stand beside and support them. In such an environment, students are often willing to take great risks—to be confronted and have some of their most cherished ideals challenged. Laurent Daloz puts the situation crisply: "What allows us, finally, to take the risk is the faith that we will survive."[10]

The pastor, of course, enjoys a trust-building environment that vastly exceeds that of the average adult educator who works in a formal setting, for the congregation is a network of relatedness that embraces the entire lives of the members. The care and love shown by the pastor in one arena of the congregation's life spills into other arenas.

Clergy earn the trust of the congregation through the careful exercise of their ministerial office: regularly communicating love for God and for the congregation; faithful pastoral care (especially pastoral calling); leading worship with uplift and planning; prompt and detailed attention to program and administrative responsibilities.[11] All these contribute directly to the climate of trust that greets teaching preachers when they step to the pulpit. The benefit of these qualities is compounded when the sermon gives evidence of thoughtful preparation. The preacher who would be a bold, creative, and imaginative teacher develops credibility through such venues as visiting the nursing home, helping the church live within its financial means, and being present at times of congregational need.

In order for the learning environment to be optimal, the members of the congregation need to feel that the church itself is a safe house. People want to know that they will not be devalued, demeaned, ridiculed, punished, or excommunicated (even informally). This needs to be communicated both orally and in the patterns of relationship and behavior in the congregation. For developing such an environment, the best point of reference for preacher and congregation is God's unconditional love for the church and the world. No idea or action—no matter how bizarre—can take us out of the realm of divine love. That love may call us to repent and change, but it never ceases to work *for* us. A circular situation comes into play here, since one of the best ways a congregation can become cognizant of this reality is to be taught with power and imagination from the pulpit.

One of the quickest ways for the teacher to erode trust is to fail to take seriously the concerns of the students. Other forms of teacherly behavior are even worse. As my colleague D. Bruce Roberts says, "It is clear that cutting, sarcastic, or combative styles of behavior in the classroom or in supervision will not support or sustain the student through the experience of risk in learning to think critically."[12] The teacher can be confrontive (and forcefully so) if the confrontation takes place in an atmosphere of trust and mutual respect.

Participation

Adult learning experiences are frequently successful when the learners participate actively in them. Participation is important on two levels.[13] At the more obvious level, adult learning events are most successful when people are actively involved in the sessions—when they can talk with one another and with the teacher, and when they do something with their bodies. For example, in a class on the use of the computer, the participants ideally would be able to raise questions and work with a computer. At a less obvious level, adults are especially receptive to learning when they have a part in planning what they will learn. Collaborative learning—when students work together in a small group on a common project—is especially attractive.[14]

Physical setting plays a role. One of the basic principles of adult learning is to provide a physical setting in which everyone—

teacher and learners—are on the same physical level. The chairs (or other physical accouterments) should be arranged so that participants can see one another face to face, not the backs of heads, as in a lecture hall. People should be grouped around tables or in conversation or activity groups.[15]

These principles would seem to work against the effectiveness of the sermon as a participatory experience. The physical arrangement of the sanctuary encourages quietism. Sanctuaries in a half-circle or in the round help people see the faces of many others, but the congregation is still regimented in rows. The service of worship is a poor setting for the Euro-American pastor to encourage verbal participation by the congregation. In addition to the disadvantage of the physical arrangement, the service usually has insufficient time for real conversation among church members.

I have never been part of a satisfactory sermon in a normal service of worship in which the preacher invited the members to respond verbally (either talking directly to the preacher or among themselves in buzz groups). People usually feel awkward and are slow to get started. Often they are asked to communicate on a personal level with people sitting near them whom they hardly know. Worse, the members often take refuge in speaking tired, unexamined platitudes or in sharing ignorance. Rather than exciting moments of discovery, such experiences often leave the participants relieved when the time of awkwardness is over. I cannot ordinarily recommend the use of verbal feedback during the Euro-American sermon.[16]

However, the sermon can become a participatory event, even with the people sitting silently in the pews. What is true of the lecture can be true also of the sermon. "An accomplished lecturer can intellectually stimulate, engage, arouse, and excite a learner's mind without the necessity for 'talking' on the part of the learner . . . there is no direct relationship between physical and intellectual passivity."[17] Silence need not denote inertia. The people can participate in the sermon in their minds and feelings and imaginations. They can listen actively and become almost as involved as if they are having cappuccino and conversation with the pastor at the cafe around the corner. If necessary, after the service, members of the congregation can seek out the pastor or other members with follow-through questions, comments, and insights.

What encourages this sense of participation? It happens when the people are drawn into the process of discovery.[18] They enter this process for various reasons. Listeners consistently become actively engaged when the sermon speaks directly to a felt *need*.[19] The congregation has an incentive to be involved when the sermon offers a *positive contribution* to their lives. Listeners tune into the preacher's frequency when they sense an important connection between the subject and *their personal or social worlds*. For instance, as a parent of five children, ages four to fourteen, the preacher immediately has my attention when a hopeful perspective on family life is offered.

The *teacher's enthusiasm* for the subject is often enough to win the interest of the congregation. Enthusiasm is infectious. I have seen people who could not spell Caesarea Philippi become absorbed with a study of its symbolism in Mark because of the preacher's fascination and energy with that subject.

The preacher can particularly help the congregation recognize and evaluate alternative understandings of a subject.[20] This encourages the congregation to feel that it is participating in the sermon as it weighs the advantages and disadvantages of each possibility. Even when the preacher recommends a particular viewpoint or action, adult learners are more likely to be receptive to that alternative when they know they have the freedom to choose another. A sermon on Joshua 6 (the collapse of the walls of Jericho), for example, might offer the listener two or three different ways of understanding that story: as a report of an event that occurred as reported; as an embellished tale with a historical kernel of truth (the Israelites captured the city and destroyed its walls); as a story whose revelatory power transcends its factual basis or nonbasis.

Listeners actively resist propaganda and manipulation. These occur when the preacher withholds or distorts information about the possible understandings of the subject, so that the congregation believes those understandings are more limited than they really are. Manipulation breeds mistrust and short circuits participation and learning. The preacher enhances the congregation's willingness to participate in the sermon and its sense of freedom by helping the members grasp the full range of possibilities for perception and behavior.

Cognitive Dissonance and Questions

Cognitive dissonance (or contradiction) is a significant impetus for adult learning.[21] This occurs when a student perceives a disparity between one mode of understanding and other possible modes of understanding. Learning is often triggered when students become aware that some of their present modes of thinking, feeling, and behaving are dissonant with some of their other thoughts, feelings, and behaviors, or with the thoughts, feelings, and behaviors of others. The students become aware of contradictions which they must resolve—within themselves, or between themselves and their worlds. Students become conscious of being in a state of disequilibrium. Aspects of their worldviews are unsettled, and they themselves may be unsettled to the point of distraction. The awareness of cognitive dissonance can trigger the students' desire to resolve the contradiction and restore a sense of life equilibrium.

Cognitive dissonance can be a teacher's best friend. As Roberts observes, "Regardless of maturity level . . . dissonance is a kind of contradiction which *facilitates growth* precisely because it creates doubt and intensifies the search for more adequate ways of understanding."[22] When people become aware of cognitive dissonance, they are often open to learning.

Cognitive dissonance can occur at different points and at differing levels of intensity. It may be as simple as my discovery that I do not possess some knowledge or skill that would be beneficial. For instance, the preacher may refer to the pool at Siloam. I do not know where the pool is located or why it is significant. Yet, in the context of the sermon, I recognize that I need to know those things; I become receptive to learning the necessary facts that make the teaching more clear. Cognitive dissonance may involve the discovery that an aspect of my worldview is inadequate.

My worldview may not account for a significant new piece of data or experience. What can I do? I can deny that such a contradiction exists. For instance, at various moments of history, occasional Christian groups have predicted that Jesus would return on a specific day. This has not happened. Yet these groups typically deny that they are in a state of contradiction. They create a rationale that reduces the dissonance. In the case of the nonarrival of Jesus, those who are disappointed might determine that while the specific date of their prediction was wrong, Jesus will return eventually (and probably soon). Ironically, the evangelistic efforts of such groups sometimes increase after the nonarrival, as the groups attempt to reduce dissonance by gathering a larger group of believers to await the return. The growth of the group therefore shows that the belief must be correct.[23]

Or I can adjust my worldview to account for the new data. In an undergraduate class in biblical literature, I sat next to a student who had grown up with very literal Bible teaching. Our assignment was to use a synopsis to compare the story of the baptism of Jesus in Matthew, Mark, and Luke.

The student next to me burst out, "Wait a minute! I always thought John baptized Jesus. That's what it says in Matthew and Mark, but in Luke it sounds like John was in prison when Jesus was baptized. Which way is it?" Gradually, she adjusted her view of the Bible to preserve its importance as a source of theological insight, while accounting for differences in interpretation of its writings.

Or, in the most radical instances, the introduction of new data can be so disruptive as to cause us to deconstruct and reconstruct major pieces of our worldview.[24] At the present time, for instance, a growing number of people realize that the modern worldview (based on the scientific method and emphasizing reason, mechanism, autonomy, and individuality) which emerged from the Enlightenment does not account for the full range of actual experience in the world. In its place, a postmodern worldview is emerging, one that integrates reason and intuition, and emphasizes relationality, dynamism, and community.[25]

One of the best ways for the preacher to initiate and continue cognitive dissonance is to pose questions to the congregation. Preachers have long used rhetorical questions to attract listener interest and serve as transition devices from one part of the sermon to another. But I am thinking now of "critical questioning" that will cause the listeners to think seriously and specifically about their values, emotions, and behavior. Stephen Brookfield notes that critical questioning is "designed to elicit the assumptions underlying our thoughts and actions. It is concerned not so much with eliciting information as with prompting reflective analysis."[26] The best questions cut to the nerve of the relationship between the subject matter and the student. Questions of this kind help to clear a space in which the learner can entertain new possibilities and perspectives.

Brookfield posits two pertinent criteria for such questions.[27] First, they should be specific. They should relate to specific persons, occasions, ideas, or practices. If preachers want to help the congregation reflect upon the relationship between providence and evil, they will not begin with questions about providence and evil in general, but about a particular situation. For instance, a forty-two-year-old woman is dying of cancer and about to leave behind a husband and three preteen children.

The preacher might ask, "What shall I say to this woman and her family? They, like many of you, believe that God is omnipotent and that God's love is unconditional and universal. Yet the mother is dying an agonizing death in her prime, at a time when her children need her desperately. What would you say to them?" The question is not hanging in a theoretical closet. The human faces of the mother and the family push the congregation to reflect upon the adequacy of their theological formula.

Second, the questions should move from the particular to the general. The questioner should begin by asking about specific situations and subsequently move to questions that deal in a more general way with the situation. After raising the specific question of what to say to the terminal cancer patient and her family, the preacher would raise the more global question of the relationship between God's love and power, and evil: "Is it possible for us to say that God is, at the same time, completely loving, completely powerful (in the sense of being able to do anything), and completely just?"

Paulo Freire and Antonio Faundez remind us that good leaders take account of the questions that are in the hearts and minds of the learners:

> Educators who do not castrate the curiosity of their students, who themselves become a part of the inner movement of the act of discovery, never show disrespect for any question whatsoever. Because, even when the question may seem to them to be ingenuous or wrongly formulated, it is not always so for the person asking it. In such cases, the role of educators, far from ridiculing the student,

is to help the student rephrase the question so that he or she can thereby learn to ask better questions.[28]

Toward this end, the preacher needs to listen for the congregation's questions and include them in the sermon. The community will be more interested in what the preacher has to say if the members believe that the preacher honors their questions and takes them into account.

Many adult learners know that life is complicated and often ambiguous. They resist simple perspectives on complex matters. They are suspicious of quick fixes of perplexing dissonances. The preacher will maintain trust and attention by acknowledging enigmas and ambiguities. Indeed, people often are willing to live with considerable uncertainty, if they sense that the community and its leader support them and will stick with them.

On some issues, it is impossible to say with confidence what is Christian and what is not. Many listeners are grateful when the preacher makes this candid admission and are willing to live in continuing uncertainty while the church continues to explore the issue.[29] During such times, the support of pastor and community is essential for the learner.

Coherence in the Content of the Subject

Learning is reinforced when students perceive coherence in the content of the subject as they encounter it from week to week. They gain confidence in their discoveries as they find that their discoveries mutually reinforce and do not contradict one another. Adult learners become suspicious when the material or conclusions of one lesson logically contradict the material or conclusions of another lesson. This suggests that they cannot count on their discoveries.

This is particularly important for preachers. In chapter 1, I called attention to research which found that from one Sunday to another, many sermons from preachers in the established denominations lack a coherent theological core. Indeed, the researcher, John McClure, found that sermons from the same pastor can be inconsistent, and even contradictory.[30] This undercuts the congregation's confidence in the message, the messenger, and ultimately, in the subject of the message (God).

Students are especially open to learning when they sense points of continuity between their own past and present, and present and future.[31] Learning, of course, often involves a change of perspective from one's past or a change of anticipation as one looks toward the future. Students are particularly willing to entertain such changes when they see that they are not completely jettisoning the past and embarking on a completely unknown future. Awareness of continuity provides a base of security upon which to realize that one's whole world will not collapse if one adopts points of view that differ from one's past or point to a future that differs from one's expectations. Awareness of continuity also assists practical steps of learning. The student can transfer (and adapt) ideas, values, and skills from the past for the present and the future.

The preacher can help the congregation welcome learning through the sermon by helping its members recognize points of continuity (as well as discontinuity) between the claims of the sermon and their current lives. Repentance, for instance, calls for changes. What arenas of my life (and of the life of our congregation) must change? And how much? On what arenas can I rely for continuing stability? What can I now expect from my future? How will repentance benefit me and my world?

Coherence extends beyond the logical relationship of the different sections of the subject matter. Some of the best teachers lead students to see how the learnings relate to the larger patterns of the learning community's knowledge, emotion, and behavior. The teacher aims for the student to see how the piece fits into the whole.

In preaching, a time-honored approach for leading the congregation to realize the global dimensions of a passage, doctrine, or topic is to ferret out its implications for individual life, for family life, for the church as community, for the local area, the state, the nation, the world. A sermon on idolatry, for example, might help us reflect on our individual idols, on how we sometimes idolize the family or the nation, on how belief in a universal transcendent God relativizes our national loyalties and awakens us to a vision of cosmic community.

The need for coherence is related to one of the most important ingredients in adult learning: the learner must take risks.[32] Adult learners need to risk thinking about new ideas, new feelings, new modes of action. Indeed, one's degree of learning is often in direct proportion to one's degree of willingness to risk. In order to take risks, students need to feel the support of the leader and of their comrades in learning. In addition, students should feel supported by a sense of continuity with their past and future. They need to feel that the promise of the new possibilities is great enough to take the risk.

Modeling Methodology for Learning and Thinking

The best teachers understand that a major part of their role is to help the learners learn how to learn.[33] Fine teachers help their students internalize both the content of the subject matter and useful methodologies, to continue their education into the subject and apply it to life outside the classroom. The teacher ought to rejoice when the student is able to work independently in the subject matter. Teachers who (even unwittingly) foster dependence in their students actually do a disservice.[34]

Teaching preachers intend to help the congregation learn how to be Christian. This includes developing Christian identity, helping the congregation to heighten its awareness of God's presence and purposes, to learn how to think theologically about all aspects of life (from the Bible through Christian history, through current issues and possibilities), and to chart how to act appropriately. Pastors do this in two ways. First, in the pulpit, they model how to learn about the Christian faith in its cognitive and experiential dimensions. For example, the pastor's exegesis and interpretation of a biblical text teaches the congregation how to engage a text. Second, from time to time, pastors can preach on how to learn and act upon the Christian faith. For instance, at the beginning of a series of sermons on current ethical issues, the pastor might preach on how Christians make ethical judgments.

One of the crucial aspects of this part of teaching and learning is that the learners must become aware of, and critical of, their own presuppositions and assumptions. These predispositions often begin with a person's own self-perception and sense of self-worth. They also include race, gender, nationality, social class, financial muscle, political affiliation, sexual orientation, intelligence, educational level, aesthetic standards, personal dress and demeanor, cleanliness, and, yes, religious commitment (or lack thereof). For instance, everyone in my circle of liberated friends would deny being racist. Most have a track record of actively supporting the African American struggle for liberation. But occasionally, I hear remarks (often quite subtle) that reveal vestiges of racism, even in the best educated and most critical of people.

Learners (and teachers) often are unaware of their attitudes about such matters. Unexamined values and attitudes can function like hidden but powerful force fields which control and limit our interactions with the subject matter, especially as it relates to our predispositions and prejudices. People often make decisions on the basis of unspoken criteria which almost automatically filter out certain options. Our possibilities for life and our freedom of choice are thereby restricted.

The teaching minister wants to help the congregation identify its presuppositions and become critical of them. The pastor also wants to encourage the congregation to become critically aware of the predispositions and hidden values of others. These "others" include the Bible, our ancestors in the Christian faith, and contemporary Christians and nonChristians. The hidden agenda is the most dangerous, especially when it sits under the altar.

Stephen Brookfield shows that the following are among the most effective approaches for helping others examine the assumptions that underlie their thoughts and actions.[35] The preacher can ask *critical questions* of the type discussed above. The preacher can use a *critical incident* as a springboard for analysis; the pastor describes an event (or a text) and leads the congregation in analyzing the nonexplicit but very powerful dimensions of the incident. For example, the preacher might lead the congregation in a reflection on the assumptions that underlie the household codes ("Wives, be submissive to your husbands") in the earliest Christian literature.[36]

The preacher can engage in *criteria analysis*—that is, helping the community name and reflect on the actual criteria it uses in self-understanding, self-evaluation (and evaluation of others), and in decision making. For instance, the church confesses that God's love is universal and unconditional. This calls for universal love toward others. But when the national interest of the United States is threatened, some Christians call for protection of that interest through violent means. The pastor can lead the congregation to consider the actual criteria that inform such perspectives.

The preacher can adapt *role-play* techniques. In an ordinary classroom setting, the teacher might assign students to play specific roles in an interactive setting, with the hope that the role playing would trigger self-awareness or other-awareness. The preacher does not have this option, but the preacher might ask the congregation to imagine what it would be like to be in a certain situation. What would it be like to live in Bosnia and have your home destroyed? How might such an awareness affect the congregation's perspective on the denomination's appeal for emergency aid for Bosnians?

Crisis-decision simulation can be especially revealing. Imagine that a nuclear explosion has hit. You are in a protected, radiation-free shelter with space for ten. Eight other people are with you. Three people come to the door and request admittance—a physician, a pregnant woman, and a teacher. You can make the decision. Which one do you admit?[37] By using such an example in a sermon, the preacher might help the community recognize the actual ways in which they value people.

Deal Creatively with Resistance

As noted in the previous chapter, congregations sometimes resist learning.[38] The preacher needs to diagnose the causes of resistance and think creatively about how to help the congregation work through it.

Why do people resist? The most common reason people resist learning can be put simply: fear of change. People long for stability, so they resist change. "In all contexts of life, we can see people for whom the threat of learning new behaviors or ideas is so unsettling that they remain in situations which will, in the long term, do them great harm."[39] For many people, predictable suffering and abuse in marriage, on the job, in a political entity, and in a thousand other arenas is preferable to the risk of the unknown.

In addition, learners may fear "cultural suicide"—that is, they fear that the change which results from learning may cut them off from their fundamental values or social group. Members of a congregation may feel that a new viewpoint is heresy. Or the learning may appear irrelevant. (Who cares whether Paul wrote I Timothy?) Or the teaching and learning styles may be disjunctive. (A call for world peace in an angry voice may be so contradictory that listeners are turned off.) Or they may be afraid of looking foolish in public. (What will our friends think when they hear what our pastor is saying about Sophia, or they see a picture in the paper of the Planned Parenthood annual banquet in our fellowship hall?) Or they may have poor self-images as learners (That's too deep for me!). Or the normal rhythm of people's learning may be to embrace new ideas, but then to retreat a bit while they soak in. They take two steps forward and one step back. The step back may be perceived as resistance. Or the students may dislike the teacher (or preacher).[40]

How can the teaching pastor help the congregation work through resistance so that the community can be free to learn?[41] Of course, there are no guarantees that the sermon can break through resistance. But Stephen Brookfield points to several possible pedagogical moves that a teacher might adapt to help the community move beyond resistance.[42] The pastor can identify the probable causes of resistance in the congregation. Is it general fear of the unknown? Or does it arise from a specific fear? Perhaps the pastor can imagine how to speak directly (or indirectly) to that fear. One of the most effective ways to allay the congregation's fears is to bring forward stories of former resisters who took the risk of learning, and then survived and prospered (see below).

Two moves sometimes go hand in hand. First, "Don't push too fast."[43] Change in human awareness usually takes place in small increments, rather than in single transformational bolts. Rather than hoping for a single sermon to convert a congregation from an antichoice position to a prochoice position (or vice versa) on the issue of abortion, for instance, the preacher might hope for an initial sermon to help the congregation think clearly about the issue without becoming incapacitated by emotionalism.

Second, preachers can explain their intentions clearly. The preacher might assure the community that the goal of the sermon is not to persuade the church to join the abortion protest on the town circle, but to open a discussion that will be going on for some time, and in which many voices and viewpoints need to be heard and weighed.

One of the best ways to transform resistance is to accentuate the positive possibilities of the new learning. When the teacher is a trusted member of the community, the learners are especially responsive to the teacher's reason for thinking the subject matter important. Brookfield posits a helpful caution here. "Be ready to describe the benefits you believe learning brings, in terms that contribute to the students' well-being, insight, and capacity for survival, rather than in terms that relate to your own concerns."[44] Before launching into an exposition of the doctrine of sanctification, for instance, a pastor might use some of the benefits of such a study to attract congregational interest.

The minister may want to name the resistance directly.[45] This is particularly useful when the community is resisting but is not aware of why it is doing so. When the source of resistance is named, it often loses its immobilizing power. At the least, the community can reflect on the cause of the resistance and on whether it is really justified. A congregation may be afraid to explore a certain subject, but may not be aware that its resistance is rooted in fear. When the pastor names fear as the source of resistance, the people then may ask, "Do we really need to be afraid of this subject?"

The preacher may be able to strike a bargain with the total resisters. The minister might concede, "Look, I know you think this is a waste of time . . ." and could then ask the congregation to at least listen to other points of view.[46]

Confrontation overcomes resistance only occasionally. I mention this because some clergy envision themselves as prophetlike figures, who blast out the blunt truth without regard for the way it will be received by their hearers. In fact, crude confrontation often only reinforces resistance. The preacher's message generally has a better chance of being welcomed if it comes in a form more friendly than confrontation. There are times, of course, when a preacher's integrity is at stake, or when a situation is so urgent that immediate decisions and actions are required. In such cases, confrontation may be the only avenue open to pastor and congregation.

If all else fails, the preacher can remember that the student has the right not only to resist learning, but to reject it altogether. The preacher needs to acknowledge this freedom and to assure the congregation that resistance will not lead to their condemnation or exile. Such acknowledgment may actually help fearful members set aside their resistance. Their sense of choice and power is thereby increased, and they may feel the freedom to experiment, at least a little bit, with new possibilities. The congregation always needs to be reminded of the goodwill of the pastor and of the pastor's continuing trustworthiness for ministry, even when the congregation's resistance interrupts the pastoral agenda.

Stories

The teaching pastor will often find that telling stories adds significantly to the learning possibilities of the sermon. This is true for several reasons. At the simplest level, well-told stories add variety and interest to the sermon. They help nourish listeners' attention. When the preacher begins to tell a story, the congregation often becomes noticeably more attentive. Some people actually lean forward in their pews. Human beings are story lovers.[47]

A story can serve as an illustration, making the point of the sermon clear and concrete. It can translate an idea into a practical life situation, with which the congregation can relate. A sermon whose purpose is to teach the members to love one another ought to contain stories that show, in practical terms, how Christians can express love.

Beyond illustration, however, good stories can bring learning to life. Good stories activate the whole self.[48] They stimulate ideas and feelings, and they lead us to imagine how we could act. Through the imagination, we experience the story much as if we are living it. The story thus becomes integrated into a listener's reservoir of experience.[49] For instance, a sermon on divine faithfulness (*hesed*) achieves its best effect if it contains a story through which the congregation experiences God's faithfulness to them.

Well-chosen stories can provide structure and meaning for our experiences. "A good story is a kind of hologram of the life of an individual, a culture, or a whole species."[50] A story can help us see how the bits and pieces of our lives come together, in a unified (or diversified) way. A narrative can integrate complexities and ambiguities into a life perspective. The stories of Genesis 1–11, for instance, locate the human family in time and space, and in relationship to transcendent life realities.

Stories of other people and communities that have made pilgrimages of discovery help the members and congregation realize that they can make similar pilgrimages and arrive unscathed. Indeed, others have taken risks that resulted in great blessing. A story often helps the congregation envision how it too might survive and be blessed. At one time, people assumed that the world was flat. But a few took the risk of believing that it might be round.

Stories are especially useful when they offer the congregation possibilities that extend beyond its immediate experience. As Laurent Daloz says, "A good story transforms our vision of the possible and provides us with a map for the journey ahead."[51] A story allows us to try out imaginatively a new perspective, a new feeling, a new behavior. This allows the congregation to venture into new areas while remaining connected to the familiar and secure.

Studies of adult education show that learning is enhanced when learners recognize that the teacher understands (and perhaps shares) their life experience.[52] Learning is further enhanced when the teacher models the risk-taking and openness that are necessary for learning.[53] Both these concerns can be addressed when *preachers tell stories of their own experiences of learning.* When did the preacher face the same issue that is before the congregation? What did the preacher think and feel? What provided the access to entertaining a change of perspective? What happened to the preacher along the route to change? And what have been the benefits (and drawbacks) of the change? The preacher's story serves as a model to show that change can safely take place.

Through the hearing of the story, the congregation participates vicariously in the preacher's journey; they experience what it would be like for them to take the same journey. If the leader is trusted, the congregation tends to be open to the new possibility. In my own life, the most powerful experiences of Christian learning have tended to come as preachers and teachers and friends have spoken of their own life journeys, fears, and transformations.

Mary Elizabeth Moore points out that hearing a story about someone else inspires the hearers to connect the story to their own lives.[54] Almost innately, the story is refracted through the listener's experience. Although the story is about someone else, I experience it as if it is happening to me. Although it is told about particular characters in particular circumstances, a story thus has the peculiar ability to speak to a generalized audience.

Learning is reinforced when students have the opportunity to test what they have learned in "real life," outside the classroom setting.[55] Learnings from the classroom and the sanctuary are solidified when the learners put them into practice in everyday life, and reflect on them. The right story, however, allows the congregation to experience aspects of that practice via the hearing of the story. The listeners imagine what it is like to live out the implications of their learning, and learning is immediately reinforced.

Thus there is a key question for the preacher: What kinds of stories best serve the purposes of a particular sermon? If the sermon is designed to add to my memory bank of biblical knowledge, can a story help to make the biblical content memorable?[56] If the sermon is intended to enrich the affective life of the congregation, can a story help the congregation feel something it has never before felt? If the sermon aims to lead the congregation into new patterns of behavior, can a story lead the congregation to experience imaginatively what it would be like to act in fresh ways?

Preachers need to be circumspect in their uses of stories. Negative stories (stories of sin, brokenness, pain, death) are much easier to find than positive stories. Yet, positive stories provide the positive visions toward which the preacher often wants the congregation to move. Therefore, the pastor must often work harder to find positive lures. As a corollary, negative stories that engage the self in its depths often have a very profound emotional impact. Indeed, a negative story sometimes can leave the listeners in such a deep hole that they cannot climb out; the story immobilizes their ability to listen to the rest of sermon. Therefore, the preacher needs to think very carefully about the placement of a powerful negative story. If it comes too early in the sermon, the listeners may be so overwhelmed that they are never able to concentrate. The preacher also needs to provide a positive story that is as emotionally and intellectually powerful as the negative one. Otherwise, the congregation is left with the implicit sense that the bad news of life is stronger than the good news. When that happens, the listeners' confidence in the preacher and in God is eroded.

Beginning and Ending the Sermon

The preacher, like the adult educator, needs to take particular account of the way the sermon begins and ends. Adults tend to remain open to a learning event, if their initial experience is "safe." They will continue to participate if they feel supported and encouraged and if they encounter the subject in an interesting way, suggesting that their time with the subject will prove beneficial. Adults are especially eager to join an event that addresses a felt need. However, if the beginning of the session is threatening, demeaning, or frightening, they tend to withdraw from active participation in the learning.[57] They may be present physically, but not psychologically.

This suggests that the beginning of the sermon ought to encourage the congregation to want to engage the complete sermon. Ordinarily, it should avoid volatile material that will inflame the listeners to the point that they do not want to interact with the material.

The particular tasks of the sermon beginning differ with the purpose of the sermon. All beginnings, of course, need to help the congregation track with the preacher into the subject matter. When the preacher approaches the pulpit, the congregation is already attentive. The preacher does not need to raise attention, but to focus it.[58] Beyond this, the preacher will be helped by asking, What does the beginning of this sermon need to do?

If the sermon is planned to introduce the congregation to a theological doctrine that sounds irrelevant and boring, the beginning may need to raise interest in the issue and suggest its pertinence to the congregation. For instance, a sermon about attending church on All Saints might begin with a humorous anecdote to highlight the misunderstanding of sainthood. For instance, the preacher might begin with the question, "What is a saint?" and then, with great exaggeration, describe a person who is perfect beyond belief. The preacher could then lightly suggest that such an idea is really a caricature. The Bible and the Christian tradition have much more believable (and achievable) notions of sainthood.

If the sermon is developed to help the congregation deal with a controversial issue, the preacher probably should avoid beginning with a statement that would immediately polarize the congregation. The pastor might, instead, start by mentioning the difficulty of talking about the subject, even among friends, and then promise not to propagandize the community, but ask the congregation to give the viewpoints in the sermon a fair hearing. Such an approach could launch a sermon on the subject of Christian uses of money in a congregation with a significant financial endowment, but whose members are divided on how to use that endowment. Before discussing how to spend the interest on the endowment, the congregation needs to understand money in a Christian perspective.

Likewise, the sermon's ending needs to encourage the congregation to continue to think about the implications of its learning.[59] The term *conclusion* is thus not always the best way to describe the end of the sermon, for *conclusion* can imply that the consideration of the subject has ended. Of course, the preacher must stop preaching. But the preacher wants the listeners to reflect upon the subject as the service continues, as they leave the sanctuary, and as they live through the week.

A story or image is often just the right stimulation for the end of the sermon. But the catalog of endings also includes friendly exhortations, questions, visions of the future, descriptions of situations in which the learning can come to life, and calls to decision (even if the decision is to keep the door of one's mind open on an issue).

When the sermon ends on a positive note, the congregation is more likely to continue ruminating on the subject. A sermon that ends negatively often leaves the congregation breathing a sigh of relief that the sermon is over. They flee from thinking about the discomfort it caused. A sermon on tithing, for instance, would short-circuit in the mind of the listener if the preacher ended with a harangue on tithing. On the other hand, the sermon would have a much better chance of receiving continued reflection if it ended by inviting the congregation to reflect on ways the practice of tithing could benefit them, the congregation's witness, and the larger community.

A small point: Many preachers end their sermons by saying "Amen." This is unfortunate. The word *Amen* is a door-closer. It cuts off learning by intimating that the final word has been spoken. I strongly recommend that pastors avoid ending sermons with "Amen." Let the sermon end with the last line.

Evaluation

The literature of adult education points out that the learning cycle is not complete until both the learner and the teacher have evaluated their mutual efforts.[60] Ideally, the evaluation of the adult learner is much more than a letter grade. The most helpful evaluation includes an assessment of the strengths and weaknesses of the learner's work, with a second round, in which the learner has an opportunity to adjust his or her performance in accordance with the suggestions of the evaluators.[61] Adult learners are most receptive to evaluation when it comes from learner peers as well as from the leader.

It is difficult for the preacher to provide evaluation of this kind in connection with the congregation's response to specific sermons. The pastor does not have a full picture of what the congregation does with the learning from the sermon in their day to day living. It takes a long time for some learning to be absorbed and expressed. A given sermon may have such a limited goal (or a goal that is carried out privately; for example, a call to early morning prayer) that it would be hard to observe its effects. But the pastor and congregation would find it illuminating when he or she prepares and preaches occasional sermons in which the pastor reflects straightforwardly with the congregation on the strengths and weaknesses of their growth in Christian faith and their common life.[62] The sermon might have the character of a "state of the church" address: What are we doing well? How are we internalizing and externalizing the lessons of the pulpit? What might we do better?

The learners also need to evaluate the leader. Someone will always compliment any sermon, but the best leaders receive evaluation graciously and will modify their performance in accordance with the serious recommendations that emerge from the process. The leaders then have their subsequent performance evaluated. Good leaders are continually being evaluated, reflecting on the evaluations, adjusting their performance, and being reevaluated.

It is difficult, of course, for congregations to offer feedback to their pastors. Few congregants know how to do so in a detailed (and diplomatic) way. The people's comments at the door on Sunday are well intended but seldom of real benefit to the preacher, as she or he seeks to upgrade the quality of communication between pulpit and pew. Further, few congregations provide useful mechanisms whereby the listeners can let the preacher know in a serious way what is getting across and what is not.

To maximize the learning climate of preaching, the preacher should devise a systematic plan for receiving responses from the congregation. The best feedback system consists of forming a small group (six to ten) of representative listeners.[63] The group meets soon after the sermon (Sunday afternoon or Monday evening) for a limited period (four to six weeks). They focus primarily on the preacher's communication style. How does the preacher's delivery and development of the content help the sermon come alive? What are the most significant things the listeners take with them from the sermon? What are the best things about the sermon and about the preacher's presence? How does the development of the content of the sermon, and its delivery, frustrate communication? What improvement would the feedback suggest?

If such groups would meet two or three times a year, the preacher would receive a significant amount of feedback. I will mention two cautions. First, the preacher must make critical judgments as to which of the group's recommendations to implement. For instance, a group might recommend an adjustment that is simply beyond the range of the preacher's personality. If such a change were made, it probably would come across as incongruous, with what the congregation otherwise knows about the preacher, and thus might erode trust.

Also, the preacher needs to avoid playing to the crowd for the sake of making the congregation comfortable or receiving good strokes in the evaluation process. For the sake of the gospel, the preacher sometimes must say things that people will not receive with immediate joy. The call to confess sin, for instance, is ultimately for the congregation's good, but immediate causes for confession are often brutal. The preacher searches for ways to help the congregation recognize the positive benefits of such confession, but cannot avoid bringing the congregation eyeball to eyeball with their sin. The pain of this recognition may not win the approval of the learning group. At such points, preachers can be assured, both by the knowledge that they are fulfilling their ordination vows and by the knowledge that learning—not necessarily an immediate feeling of satisfaction in the learner—is the goal of adult education.[64]

When the most proven principles of adult education are incorporated into the sermon, they often enhance learning. However, the preacher has no guarantee that drawing upon these principles will lead to success. Due to circumstances beyond the preacher's control (or even awareness), the best prepared sermons sometimes are dead even before they are spoken. Another sermon may seem so ill-conceived that the preacher is ashamed to deliver it, but it strikes fire. Nonetheless, the *average* quality of communication between pulpit and pew typically rises as preachers become more self-conscious about developing sermons that make use of the best of what we know about how people learn and mature.

C H A P T E R • 4

Developing the Sermon As an Event of Teaching and Learning

The monthly meeting of the central administrative body of the congregation ends. On the parking lot, you finally say good-bye to those people who inevitably stay late. You get into your car. You reflect on the meeting as the soft green lights from the instrument panel envelop you. The Stewardship Committee recommended allocations for world outreach, for the shelter for the homeless, and for the local hospice for AIDS patients. But several on the board protested.

As you recall the words of protest, you wonder, "How could a Christian think that way?" Their ideas sound as though they came from a popular but narcissistic radio talk show, not from the Bible or Christian doctrine or faithful practice. As you pause at a long stoplight, you think of other things that people say and do that are out of place in the Christian house. Good people. Well intentioned. They want to be faithful. But clearly, they need to enlarge their consciousness of Christian identity and mission. And you flinch as you realize gaps in your own Christian thought and life.

You want to help the congregation deepen its Christian awareness and practice. You know that it will take more than a sermon or two to encourage the community to mature. In fact, if you take up the subject in only one sermon, you may be asking for unproductive conflict. But you are confident that preaching can play an important role in such movement. How, then, do you develop a sermon that is intended to be an event of teaching and learning?

This chapter outlines some basic considerations for developing a teaching sermon. We first focus on clarifying what needs to be taught. Subsequently, we identify resources that can inform a sermon in light of the specific needs of the congregation. We consider directions for a given sermon (or series of sermons). The chapter concludes with a discussion of possibilities for shaping the sermon so that it has a good opportunity to spark growth in the congregation.[1] Appendix A contains a sample worksheet that might be of help when working through the following steps toward a teaching sermon.

A systematic approach to developing the sermon can help the preacher cover the many bases that need to be touched. A plan for preparation often helps me remember to pay attention to information and issues that I could easily overlook. However, a systematic approach is also dangerous. The system of preparation (or the pastor's predisposition) may cause the preacher to overlook aspects of the subject that are important and challenging. These may allow the pastor to prejudge the material, to the extent that the possibility of fresh discovery (even for the teacher) disappears in a room of stale familiarity. They may short-circuit the encounter of the preacher and congregation with the potentially electric issue. Hence, the pastor needs always to be critical of the process of preparation itself.[2]

Identify a Point at Which the Congregation Needs to Learn

The teaching preacher often begins by reflecting systematically on the life of the community and identifying something the congregation needs to learn about the Christian faith and its interpretation of life and (or) its implications for behavior.[3] Consider this as a focusing question: *What do we, as a congregation, most need to learn this week (and in the coming weeks and months) as a part of our growth in Christian understanding and action?* The need may call for a single sermon, or it may require a series of sermons over the next few weeks, or it may be addressed best by a long-range plan, in which the preacher returns to this need once every month during the next several months.

The congregation may be conscious of this need, or it may not. If heavy rains have caused a flash flood that wiped out several homes along the river, the congregation may yearn to understand God's relationship to natural disaster. However, in the story at the beginning of this chapter, several members of the central administrative body of the congregation believe that their notions of Christian identity and mission are airtight. They need to have some fresh air blown through the windows of their minds, but they do not recognize this need.

Foci for learning can be as various as life. In order to think systematically about things the congregation needs to learn, a preacher might review arenas of existence. In Leander Keck's vivid phrase, the preacher is a "priestly listener" to the life of the congregation and the culture.[4] What is happening in the larger culture that can become an entry point for discussion of the gospel and of how the gospel instructs us to perceive and act? In the city, town, or neighborhood? In Christian doctrine? In the congregation as community? In the lives of parishioners or in the pastor's own life? When moving toward a teaching sermon, the preacher will seek to show how the gospel shapes our understanding and response to these situations, issues, and questions.

Some clergy survey their congregations periodically. In written form, they ask the congregation, "What is on your heart and mind that you would like to have interpreted in a sermon during the next year (or half year or quarter)?" This approach allows the congregation to voice the needs it feels and often uncovers interests that otherwise are hidden from the preacher.

The use of a lectionary provides many preachers with a predetermined starting point, and there are significant reasons for this.[5] A foundational principle of a lectionary is that its themes, texts, and seasons are constitutive of Christian identity. It portrays the normative Christian vision in several (though not all) of its dimensions. When the teaching preacher begins with a lectionary text, there is a key starting question: What do we most need to learn from this text, in the context of the season of the year in which it is found? The pastor may review categories such as the ones described above, in light of the seasonal emphasis of the text. How does our learning from this text help us interpret the larger culture? Our city, town, or neighborhood? Our congregation as community? The lives of people I know? My own life?

On Epiphany, for instance, the church remembers the manifestation to the Gentiles of God through Jesus. What do we most need to learn from the story of the pagan astrologers coming to the infant Jesus? (Matt. 2:1-12). In Matthew, this story points to the Gentile mission. The preacher may conclude that the congregation needs to be reminded that God's grace is still freely poured out to persons and communities whom the contemporary church regards as "gentile."

The great strength of a lectionary is that it reminds the preacher that proactively, the gospel ought to shape the congregation's vision and life. The sermon is not simply an occasion to show how the gospel answers needs felt by a congregation. A lectionary represents the church's foremost need—to understand itself and the world in terms of the gospel. From the perspective of the gospel, we recognize our true needs. But a lectionary does not always provide the best biblical or theological material to address a particular moment or situation. The lectionary preacher needs to exercise critical judgment on the timeliness of readings and situations, and feel free to preach beyond the lectionary if the occasion calls for it.

Pastors may not be able to identify one need that rises above all others. Several possibilities may seem equally important. In such cases, they may take comfort in the fact of preaching forty-eight sermons a year. To adapt a quote from Ernest T. Campbell, "Every Sunday is not Armageddon."[6] A subject postponed this week may be addressed another time. When faced with multiple opportunities with equal claims, the preacher might pick the one that most excites her or him. Sometimes the preacher's energy for the subject creates energy for it in the congregation.

Determine the Basic Issues and Questions Essential for Understanding and Preaching on the Subject

I find it immensely helpful to make a list of the basic issues and questions that are essential in preparing a sermon for teaching and learning; these are fundamental matters for the interpretation of the subject.[7] What do I, as preacher and as learner (and the congregation as learning community), most need to know and experience, to be in a position to come to a fulsome Christian understanding? Often these issues will help the preacher become acquainted with the subject in the past (its history), in the present (its current manifestations) and in the future (how shall we understand it or act on it in the coming days, weeks, years?).

When developing a sermon on a biblical text, for instance, I need to research the text from the standpoints of historical, literary, and theological exegesis.[8]

Some sample questions might include: What is the historical setting (if known)?; the literary context?; the meaning of the vocabulary?; the genre and its function?; the effect of the text on the reader?; the theological witness of the text?; the instructivity (or lack thereof) of that witness for today?

If the sermon is to introduce the congregation to a Christian notion of prayer, the questions might include: What is the definition of prayer?; how has prayer been understood and practiced in the Bible and in the Christian community across the years?; what is the purpose of prayer today?; what can the congregation expect from God when the members pray?; what effect does prayer have on those who pray? And how do we pray?; what words do we use?; what are some unhelpful, or even false, understandings of prayer?; how does one develop a life of prayer?

As a part of African American History Month, the preacher might bring the gospel to bear on racism: What do we mean by race?; racism?; when did racism emerge in human affairs?; how is it manifest in the world of the Bible and in Christian history?; when (and why) did racism become associated with skin color?; why does racism persist?; what does it feel like to be the object of racist behavior, to live in a culture with racist overtones?; how does God value people of different races?; how should Christians value people of different races?; what makes it possible for a person to repent of racism and seek beloved community?; what does God desire in relationships among the races? Should the racial communities and cultures today set aside their distinctive qualities and seek to become a large homogenous body (on the model of the melting pot), or should they seek ways to encourage their individuality, while learning to live together in mutual support and encouragement? What practical steps can people, congregations, and cities take to move toward a gospel vision of community?

Investigate Resources Needed to Understand the Subject

The preacher should prepare carefully for the teaching sermon in order to present the subject with clarity, depth, and power, so that it makes a maximal witness to the gospel. The learner's trust in the learning event increases in direct proportion to the learner's perception of the knowledge, thoroughness, and fairness of the leader. The preacher's integrity is at stake, and she or he wants to tell the whole truth. Careful preparation calls for thorough investigation of sources of knowledge that can help both pastor and congregation come to an adequate grasp of the subject.

When developing the teaching sermon, clergy might find it helpful to investigate resources in four areas. First is the *Bible,* and when using the Bible, there is simply no substitute for also using the best concordances, Bible dictionaries, commentaries, and other interpretive helps. The preacher wants to hear a text in its own voice.

When preaching from a lectionary passage or from a freely chosen biblical text, the Bible sets a major part of the agenda for the sermon: What does this text need to teach us today?

But when preaching from biblical texts, preachers need to be careful not to limit their fields of reflection and investigation to a particular passage. (Some preachers are so devoted to "preaching the text" that they effectively make the text an idol, shutting off conversation with other texts and sources of theological insight that could enrich the congregation). The witness of a text sometimes needs to be amplified, supplemented, or corrected by other texts, by the history of how the text has been used in the church, and by resources such as the others listed below.

When the sermon starts at a point other than the text, the preacher needs to be careful to honor the fullness of the biblical witnesses in their historic and literary contexts. The subtle temptation, when a sermon starts with a doctrine or topic, is to use biblical passages as proof texts.

A second body of resources is *the history of the church* (and perhaps beyond the church), from the close of the canon into the present. What are the most important ways in which the subject has been understood? These perspectives often help the preacher see how Christian views have been clarified, deepened, applied, distorted, even have been destructive. Such information is fascinating in its own right. Further, it often provides the preacher with perspectives that are useful in the sermon, particularly when a voice from the past helps to sort out a contemporary perspective on the subject. While it may seem daunting to review the history of the church's grasp of the subject, the pastor can often turn to dictionaries of the Bible, books on church history, theology, ethics, worship, education, and preaching, to find concise overviews of the subject.

A third body of resources can be classified as *contemporary studies* of the subject. The preacher can often be helped by investigations in psychology, sociology, economics, politics, ecology, and the natural sciences, as well as by the reflections of contemporary theologians, ethicists, and teachers. Usually, these can be located by a trip to the local public library.

The recommendation to turn to these resources is accompanied by a danger. While our culture no longer lionizes the sciences in quite the way it did in the middle of the twentieth century, empirical investigation is still highly prized. In such an atmosphere, it is easy for the preacher, often unconsciously, to let these materials take over the sermon without bringing them into dialogue with theological witness and reflection. It also is easy for clergy to misrepresent or oversimplify such analyses. When this happens, the credibility of the sermon comes into question.

A fourth body of resources resides in the *arts*. Often, the preacher will find sensitive illumination of the subject in cinema, in a past or present novel, in a poem, in a painting or other media. The artist may alert pastors to dimensions of the subject they had not seen before. The artistic medium may allow the preacher and the congregation to experience the subject in ways that enlarge cognitive understanding. An added benefit: The preacher may be able to use the artistic material directly in the sermon.

Potential problems come to the surface in connection with the use of the arts. A preacher cannot turn to the arts with the ease that one turns to a Bible dictionary. I cannot simply run down the street to the Indianapolis Museum of Art and look up a painting on tithing. Therefore, a pastor may want to keep a notebook with a record of artistic experiences, events, and sources.[9] (Before *The Teaching Sermon* goes out of print, however, preachers who have access to the Internet will be able to access a remarkable number of databases).

Another problem is aesthetic cannibalism. I sometimes come upon an artistic expression with homiletical possibilities. Immediately I think, "Ah, this might fit into a sermon." Instead of letting the aesthetic experience happen in its own way, I scavange it for the way I can use it in a sermon. This reduces my own encounter with the piece, and hence reduces the depths with which the piece can speak through the sermon to the congregation. It sometimes violates the integrity of the expression itself.

Pastors make the best use of the arts in sermon preparation when they experience the arts for their own sake, in everyday living (e.g., in the process of going to the movies or the concert hall or the art gallery). And when referring to artistic material in the sermon, the preacher usually is advised not to draw out the lesson or moral. Usually, the artistic expression can have its best effect in the sermon (as in ordinary life) by being allowed to make its own point in its own way. The arts teach best by being experienced, not by being explained.[10] As indicated in the previous chapter, a teaching sermon can be an aesthetic experience. Some preachers, in fact, are developing multimedia sermons which incorporate images on screens, short dramas, brief moments of dance, or other modes of aesthetic expression.

A sidenote: The pastor needs to honor the complexities and ambiguities that may turn up in this investigation. For instance, on some subjects, the preacher will uncover empirical research that comes to different conclusions about how to interpret the data and the subject. The preacher may decide that one interpretation is superior to the others. But in the sermon, it is important to acknowledge such difficulties, and to give both the strengths and the weaknesses of one's own conclusion. Such acknowledgment is important in the interest of accuracy and fairness. It shows the investigator's integrity. It increases the congregation's trust in the preacher. And it also signals the congregation that the teacher honors the listeners' ability to think for themselves. This is essential, for adult learners resist attempts at manipulation, or signs that the teacher does not respect them or their capacities.

Come to a Christian Understanding of the Subject

The preacher needs to come to a clear understanding of the subject that is coherent with the gospel. This requires sifting through the data gathered above and weighing it against the gospel and its norms. Though the theological vision of the church can be stated in different ways, Clark Williamson, a systematic theologian, summarizes the essence of Christian faith:

> The church lives by and from the proclamation of the gospel, the good news that God graciously and freely offers the divine love to each and all (oneself included) and that this God who loves all the creatures therefore commands that justice be done to them. This dipolar gospel (a) *promises* God's love to each of us as the only ground of our life, and (b) *demands* justice from us toward *all* whom God loves. God's justice and God's love are the two modes of expression of the one divine character, God's *hesed*.[11]

The church learns of God's love through Jesus Christ. This vision is the core of the church's teaching.

The gospel embraces humankind and nature as it stresses God's love for every created entity. It focuses our attention on God's grace, as gospel songs put it, "for *even* me." Yet it guards against cheap grace by reminding us that it is necessary for us to respond to divine grace with justice. At the same time, it guards against works-righteousness by helping us to acknowledge that our works of justice and love do not win divine favor for us, but are necessary expressions of who we are—that is, the beloved of God.

The church has a practical theological way to relate this vision to its life and witness. The church can ask three questions of every phenomenon it encounters, from a biblical text to a church doctrine, to a historical recollection, to a personal action or social situation, or to a theological statement:[12]

1. Is it *appropriate to the gospel*—that is, does it manifest God's love for all? Racial intolerance, for instance, is inappropriate because it denies God's love for all.

2. Is it *intelligible*? Intelligibility involves two sub-themes. The first is consistency with other things that Christians say and believe, as measured by the norm of appropriateness. It is not intelligible to believe or act in contradictory ways. One cannot be

consistent if one confesses that God wills justice for all, but leads a church that oppresses women.

The other sub-theme has to do with worldview. Is a Christian interpretation of a facet of life consistent with the way we understand the world today?[13] From the standpoint of what we know about the capabilities of women and men today, it does not make sense to say that women are so constituted that they need to be ruled by men.

3. Is it *moral*—that is, does it call for behavior that demonstrates God's unreserved love for each and all?

For example, a pastor begins developing a sermon on Ephesians 1:3-15. The exegesis of the text leads her to consider the possibility of universal salvation. Broadening her study from the specific text to the larger question of universal salvation, she finds material both to support and to deny universal salvation elsewhere in the Bible, in church history, and in contemporary theology. The pastor then asks these key questions:

a. Is universal salvation *appropriate to the gospel* of God's unconditional love for each and all, and God's unremitting will for justice for each and all? Yes, she decides. Indeed, what could be more appropriate? If God saved some, but not others, then God's love would not be universal or unconditional.[14] If God denies salvation to some, then God does not act justly—that is, God does not do what is right, according to God's own character (which is universal, unconditional love).

b. Is universal salvation *intelligible?* Again, her answer is affirmative, in light of both sub-themes of this criterion. Universal salvation is consistent with other things that Christians believe about God's unconditional love and will for justice. Of course, the preacher must deal carefully with other passages and voices in the Christian tradition that do not support universal salvation. And the preacher must come to a clear understanding of the meaning of salvation itself.

c. Is universal salvation *morally plausible?* Yes. However, many in the congregation will perceive universal salvation as a challenge to their ordinary ways of thinking and relating. Many people want to affirm the value and worth of persons who are good citizens, but they want wrongdoers to be punished. How does the notion of universal salvation affect this eye-for-an-eye mentality? Is it right to say that the Hitlers of the world are saved?

Once in a while, a pastor will work through a subject that does not yield a clear Christian interpretation. It may be enigmatic as to what is fully appropriate to the gospel, intelligible, or morally plausible. In such cases, the preacher might share these ambiguities with the congregation. As mentioned in the previous section, honesty and preservation of the congregation's trust call for this. The preacher can still work through the subject and analyze points of relative appropriateness and inappropriateness, intelligibility and nonintelligibility, moral plausibility and implausibility. The preacher may need to help the congregation learn to live patiently with these relativities while awaiting further clarification.[15]

Describe the Congregation's Relationship to the Subject

It will help preachers to think through possibilities for developing the sermon if they have a sense of how the congregation is related to the subject. How does the community think, feel, and act with respect to the subject? The following categories (and others that the pastor may identify) may help assess the particular needs of the community. Such analysis may be helpful later in weighing the possibilities of different homiletical approaches for teaching and learning.

A congregation may be *informed and enthusiastic*. A listener might think, "I know about this. I like it! I want to do more with it."

A congregation may be *favorably inclined toward the subject but have an inadequate understanding or experience of the subject*. Or the listeners *may not know how to act in response to the subject:* "I am interested in this. I don't know much about it, but I am open to the possibility of greater understanding, experience, or guidance for action." Perhaps the congregation has forgotten what it once knew or experienced. However, in today's church, the preacher needs increasingly to examine the possibility that the congregation has never known or experienced the subject in a fulsome way.

The listeners may be *informed about or have experience in the subject, but act out of character:* "I know about the subject, but I don't do anything about it, or (consciously or unconsciously) I act against it." The people know who they are and what is true, but they behave contrary to their own identity and beliefs. The preacher will be helped by thinking about why the community is in a state of contradiction. It may be apathetic or resistant, as in the following categories.

The listeners may be *apathetic* about the subject: "I don't care" (yawn). They may be informed but uncaring. They may have inadequate understanding or experience of the subject and no interest in it. Apathy may reflect a simple lack of concern, or it can be a manifestation of passive resistance.

The listeners may be *unfavorably inclined, even resistant to new possibilities of perception, experience, or action:* "I don't like this, and I don't really want to know about it." The congregation may have little information or it may have misinformation. Either way, it resists interaction with the subject. Some listeners may actively resist becoming involved. Others may passively resist. Seasoned pastors with whom I have discussed this subject report that in many communities, passive resistance is the most common form of congregational resistance to new possibilities for thought, emotion, or activity. Few people actively fight the preacher, but, like the passive-aggressive personality, many resist by not responding.

Of course, a congregation probably will have people in each of these categories. But the pastor usually can locate a point at which the tide of congregational opinion and feeling rises to the most common crest—more people gather around this viewpoint than around the others. It is likely that the preacher will want to prepare the sermon to speak especially to these people, but also will need to think how to include those from other viewpoints, either in the sermon itself or elsewhere in the service.

Determine What You Hope Will Happen
as a Result of Hearing the Sermon

The preacher determines what she or he hopes will happen in the minds, hearts, and actions of the congregation, as a result of participating in the sermon.[16] The goal for the sermon results from the investigation of the subject and from the analysis of the congregation. It also takes into account the "sermon in a sentence," as described in the next section of this chapter. Soon, the pastor will think through the form and content of the actual sermon. How can I speak so that the sermon might have the best chance of accomplishing its goal? But first, the preacher should be clear about what the sermon needs to do. The learning event of the sermon is shaped according to its purpose.

If the congregation is largely uninformed about the subject, the sermon probably will need to provide, creatively and invitingly, the requisite information and help the congregation understand how this information (and responding appropriately to it) can make a positive addition to its life. If the congregation knows about the subject, but is apathetic, the sermon might create an experience of the subject, designed to help the congregation feel some passion for it. If the community is informed but does not act as it should, the sermon probably will try to persuade it to see the connection between its insight and its behavior: "Since we are this way . . . then we act this way."

If the congregation is misinformed or misbehaving, the preacher may want the sermon to help the listeners recognize their points of misfit and see the advantages of new perspectives, deeper feelings, more apropriate actions. If the congregation resists the subject, the preacher probably will want to work at overcoming the resistance, attempting to maintain the goodwill of the listeners (if possible) while encouraging them to consider new ways of thinking, behaving, emoting. If the congregation is enthusiastic and informed, the preacher may want to help it envision ways to extend the implications of its perspective into new arenas of perception or action.

Can a sermon point the congregation in the direction of discovering or rediscovering more than one thing? Of course. A congregation that is decidedly mixed in its relationship to the subject may require multiple aims. However, the more goals for a sermon, the harder it is to keep the points of the sermon working together as a single pulse toward discovery or experience.

A qualifier: Once the sermonic event is underway, the preacher cannot control what happens. At best, a preacher can plan so that the sermon has a good opportunity to accomplish its purpose. The church may learn precisely what the preacher has in mind. But the chemistry of the community may be such that the sermon interacts with the people in a way differently than imagined. The sermon can take on a life of its own. The pastor can only give glory to God when the sermon unexpectedly strengthens the community. At other times, the preacher may need to exercise damage control. My experience is that parishioners who react with unanticipated aggravation are often quite understanding when I explain, "What you heard was not what I intended. I was trying to say. . . ."

Summarize the Content of the Sermon in a Single Indicative Sentence

In teaching sermons, preachers should be as clear as possible about what to say and what they hope the congregation discovers as a result of joining in the sermon. The pastor articulates the particular theological content of the sermon and the help it offers the congregation. What is the *specific* way this sermon seeks to help the congregation name the world (and its experience in the world) in the terms of the gospel? What does the congregation learn from this biblical text (or this Christian doctrine, or this Christian understanding of a topic) that will help its Christian life and witness?

Every preaching textbook known to me recommends that the pastor make a clear statement of the central focus of the sermon.[17] This is the distillation of the theological lesson or experience which the preacher hopes the congregation will discover through the sermon. I call this statement the *sermon-in-a-sentence*—it puts the content of the sermon into a single sentence. The sentence may never actually be stated in the sermon, but, depending on the purpose of the sermon, the sermon amplifies it, considers questions it evokes, creates emotional associations, brings it to bear on individuals and communities, thinks through its implications for thought, action, feelings.

Because the sermon hopes to teach the congregation good news about God for the world, this sentence has a positive character.[18] As shown in the following diagram, the subject is God. Its verb would be an activity of God. Its predicate would indicate a result of God's presence or activity and, perhaps, our response:

Subject	Verb	Predicate
God	An activity of God	A result of God's activity and our response.

For instance, if the preacher is preparing a teaching sermon on Genesis 21:1-7 (the birth of Isaac), the sermon-in-a-sentence might be, "God is faithful to us, even as God was faithful to Abraham and Sarah." The preacher might want the congregation to learn the meaning of faithfulness and experience God's faithfulness imaginatively through the sermon, to consider the way God is faithful even in the midst of circumstances that seem to deny that faithfulness.

The sentence is nearly always indicative in character—that is, it states the way things *are* between God and us. It stresses God's initiatives in behalf of the world. This is theologically appropriate. The sermon-in-a-sentence is practically never imperative. God does not first demand from us. God first reminds us of who we are (the beloved) and then reminds us of the way we should live in response.

A positive sermon-in-a-sentence attracts the congregation (much like honey in the flower attracts the bee) to accept its learning in a positive and inviting way. As a learner, I want to accept this lesson. An imperative, on the other hand, often imposes a burden. It seldom provides the power to fulfill its own demand; listeners feel frustrated and impotent rather than called to obedience. In the worst instances, the imperative drifts into works-righteousness.

Does this mean that the preacher never talks about the congregation's moral responsibility and always avoids bad news? Certainly not! Sometimes the congregation must admit its inaction or misdeeds, its own sin and complicity in evil, if the listeners are to grow in faith and practice. These misperceptions need to be named and owned. However, to be faithful to the gospel and enhance the learning climate, the preacher usually should approach these negative realities in a framework of God's renewing presence and activity. The preacher may begin with the good news and go to the bad, then return to the good. Or the preacher may move from the bad to the good. But whatever the specific movement, the sermon should leave the listeners assured, empowered, and with a positive vision for the future.

List the Questions and Other Matters Likely to Be on the Hearts and Minds of the Listeners as They Intersect with the Sermon

The preparation of the teaching sermon will be helped if the preacher lists the questions, issues, experiences, and other associations that are likely to be a part of the congregation's intersection with the subject. These are a part of the ecology within which the congregation will participate in the sermon. If the preacher does not take these matters into account, their absence from the sermon can leave the congregation dissatisfied and inattentive. Learners are more receptive to the learning event when they recognize their concerns in the event. If the preacher does not address these concerns, the congregation may be left with the impression that its preexisting judgments, experiences, or behaviors exhaust the subject. Further, the preacher may be able to use such material directly (or indirectly) in the sermon.

How does the teaching minister obtain the material for such a list? The preacher can engage in "priestly listening"—that is, listening to the members to hear what is on their hearts and minds.[19] The pastor may remember comments that people have made in meetings or during pastoral calls, or members of the community may be interviewed. If the congregation includes a group of people who help the pastor with sermon preparation (for example, a lectionary study group), they might be asked to verbalize their own points of contact, questions, issues, feelings. The preacher could take stock of his or her own associations with the subject; if the preacher has questions, problems, issues, concerns, or experiences, some in the congregation may have these as well. The pastor could try to imagine how different people in the listening community might respond to the subject. This sometimes yields very different perspectives that need to be included in the breadth of the sermon.

The news media and artists sometimes point the pastor toward matters that are consciously or unconsciously in the listening environment.

Pastors frequently will find it illuminating to inventory their own experience with the subject. How have I encountered it? What have I been taught about it? How do I feel about it? How do I act in respect to it? How do these experiences shape my own interaction with the subject? Am I similar to—or different from—the community? Such an inventory will nearly always turn up material which the minister can use directly in the sermon, particularly if the sermon asks for a change of perception. Often, clergy can use the factors that contributed to a change in themselves to help the congregation envision change in themselves: "I used to be that way . . . but then I discovered . . . and now I am this way."

For instance, a pastor is preparing a sermon on the doctrine of justification by grace through faith. The list of questions grows quickly. What is the definition of justification; of grace; of faith? What role does faith play in justification? If one does not have faith, is one not justified? Is a person justified without faith? We live in a culture based on the principle of works-righteousness (what is that?). From the very beginning of our lives, we are taught to work, work, work, to prove and improve ourselves. How can people who live with such a worldview accept the doctrine of justification by grace?

What do we do in response to the news that we are justified by grace through faith; what are the practical consequences of this knowledge? How does this doctrine help people on a day to day basis? The preacher thinks of people for whom faith functionally becomes a work—that is, something they do that makes God favorably inclined toward them. How should it affect the members' views of others, if they viewed one another as justified? How should it affect the congregation's view of the gang of kids that keeps spray painting its logo on the church building, if the congregation viewed them as already justified?

I find it useful to keep this list of questions and issues on my desk. Periodically, as I am working on the sermon, I ask myself, "Am I taking account of these matters in the sermon itself?" The material can be expressed in different ways. A preacher might raise these themes in the congregation's own words, or might tell a story or incident that allows the congregation to recognize its issues, or might ask a congregation its own question: Isn't this promise too good to be true? Or pastors might articulate a point of contact through their own experience: "Something about this text bothers me. I wonder if it bothers you." A citation from an article, book, newspaper, or media presentation might provide a good venue for helping the congregation recognize its particular pieces of the puzzle in the sermon.

Plan the Content and Movement of the Sermon so that Listeners Have a Good Opportunity to Learn What They Need to Learn

The preacher develops a specific plan, so that the content and movement of the teaching sermon can work together to give the congregation an opportunity to encounter the subject in a positive way. The pastor takes account of the congregation's relationship to Christian understanding of the subject, the congregation's questions and issues pertinent to the subject, and what the pastor hopes will happen as a result of participating in the sermon. How can the preacher work with the flow of the congregation's conciousness and feelings to maximize the likelihood for a positive intersection with the subject (and to minimize the likelihood for distortion or hostility)? Teaching methods and potential outcomes for the sermon often can be suggested by the ecology of the community's attitude toward the subject. A plan for teaching and learning that would be apropos in one setting might not work as well in another, because the ecologies of the listening communities would be different.

The easiest sermonic situation occurs when the congregation is *informed and enthusiastic*. The preacher does not need to provide remedial information, perspective, or experience. The sermon can build on a base of awareness and ride the congregation's stream of energy into new or deeper vistas. The pastor's basic work is to help the congregation focus its interest and goodwill. The sermon might begin by naming and tapping into the community's positive association with the subject, then helping the congregation imagine the next steps in growth in its relationship with the subject: "We are

Callslip Request 6/4/2012 7:57:46 AM

Request date:5/31/2012 11:44 AM
Request ID:34803
Call Number:251 AL428T
Item Barcode:

Author: Allen, Ronald J. (Ronald James),
Title: Teaching sermon / Ronald J. Allei
Enumeration:c.1

Patron Name:Erin Hollaar
Patron Barcode:

Pickup Location:

Request number:

Route to:
I-Share Library:

Pick-up Location:

excited about this. What do we do next?" In a congregation that has resolved an internal conflict and is in the excitement of rekindled life as a community, the preacher may assess some possibilities for new forms of expressing their commitment.

The preacher faces a slightly different challenge when the community is *favorably inclined toward the subject but has an inadequate understanding or experience of the subject, or does not know how to act in response to the subject.* The preacher still can assume the favorable disposition of the listeners toward the topic. The sermon can plunge into the subject directly, but en route, needs to help the congregation recognize the deficiencies of its awareness or action and urge it toward fuller comprehension or activity.

The pastor asks, "Given the mood of the congregation, how can I help it discover the information or have the experiences, and resolve to behave in ways that are essential to this subject?" For one congregation, straightforward critical reflection may be an optimum plan; the preacher gets the congregation on board, explains that it has a view that is only partially correct, identifies weaknesses, and points toward the benefits of a revitalized perception. In another setting, a more subtle approach may be needed.

For instance, a passage from the book of Revelation appears in the lectionary. The congregation is interested in the meaning of that book. Many have never read it and bring only curiosity to the sermon. Others, whose interest has been sparked by friends who attend churches which espouse premillennialism, have been influenced by that view but are not deeply committed. They are vague premillennialists because they have never encountered another way of thinking. The pastor's priestly listening has revealed that several key thinkers in the community have questions about this viewpoint. The pastor then explains the strengths and weaknesses of premillennialism as informed by historical criticism, which posits another mode of interpreting the book of Revelation that is just as hopeful and practical.

After the sermon, a leading elder gushes, "Gosh, I always wanted to think that way, but until now, I didn't know it was possible."

Similar dynamics may be at work when the congregation is *informed about or has experience with the subject, but acts out of character.* The community is interested in the subject and has a good grasp of it, but does not act on its knowledge. The congregation needs to understand that identity ought to lead to behavior that is consistent with that identity and knowledge. The congregation simply has not made the connection (or has forgotten the connection) between these matters. The preacher probably can raise the subject, point out the discrepancy, and help the congregation consider appropriate action.

For example, the congregation at Old First affirms that God's love, and the church, are truly ecumenical. But when the pastor of the congregation down the street was implicated in sexual misconduct, many in the congregation chuckled and took a slightly superior view of the situation. Some even told jokes that cast that pastor in a demeaning light. In the sermon, the preacher at Old First reminds the congregation of the width of the real ecumenicity of the church. The preacher acknowledges differences between Old First and the strict congregation down the street, but attempts to help the congregation understand that members of a truly ecumenical community ought to respond with compassion and sensitivity toward their companions in Christ down the street (while not condoning the misconduct or endorsing the other congregation's theological vision).

Some cases of discontinuity between what a congregation knows and what it ought to be, feel, or do are more difficult. This is particularly true when the congregation is either actively or passively resistant to the subject. We discuss these possibilities later, in connection with a congregation's unfavorable inclination toward the subject.

The homiletical task takes on a slightly different character when the community is *apathetic*. The people have not forgotten the subject. They have had opportunities to know about it. Perhaps some have even absorbed its substance. But they do not care about it. The preacher's calling is to help the congregation develop a desire to engage the subject. The preacher asks, "What questions, data, stories, or points of connection might strike a spark in the kindling of the congregation's mind or heart?"

I know a pastor whose congregation was notoriously apathetic toward the mission offering for One Great Hour of Sharing. The pastor's priestly listening to the congregation indicated that the people did not feel a personal connection to this offering. In previous years, the rationale for the offering had been presented to the congregation through charts and statistics, for the purpose of meeting the goal established for the congregation by the denomination. The preacher planned a short series of sermons to put a human face on the purpose of the offering. The preacher taught that the offering is grounded in divine compassion for the world, that human compassion is the proper response, and then recounted vignettes of persons who would be aided by the offering. The offering increased from $350 the previous year to $1,700, and has kept climbing in subsequent years.

The most difficult preaching challenge is the congregation that is *unfavorably inclined, even resistant to new possibilities of perception, experience, or action.* Those who actively resist the subject are relatively easy for the preacher to identify. Their remarks or actions exhibit their attitudes. During the sermon, they may glower or even stomp out of the sanctuary. They may communicate with the preacher directly after the service. In the current church, the subject of abortion often arouses such resistance. While active resistance is often enervating for clergy, some have the advantage of knowing where the people stand, and therefore of being able to think clearly about potential homiletical and pastoral response, both immediately and in the long term.

Others may passively resist a subject. Their disinterest or disagreement is silent. They exhibit their disinclination through disinterest or unresponsiveness. Priestly listening can sometimes clue the preacher in to the possibility of passive resistance. Such people may show few signs that the preacher can easily spot while preparing the sermon. Sometimes, in fact, the first clue to such passivity is the congregation's response (or lack thereof) to the sermon. This, of course, becomes data that can be critical to the preparation of another sermon on that subject at a later time.

For instance, a Euro-American congregation plans a joint service with an African American congregation to celebrate the birthday of Martin Luther King, Jr. In preparation for that occasion, the Euro-American pastor preaches from Dr. King's legacy to a congregation of 127. The congregation receives the sermon with no visible response. But when the joint service takes place, only 14 Euro-Americans are present. This turnout suggests passive resistance.

Those who resist may have well-thought-out reasons for not dealing with a subject, or they may be aware of emotions that raise more pain than they are willing to face when the subject arises. They may have deeply entrenched but unconscious ideas, values, social relationships, vested interests, or fears that discourage them from wanting to risk new possibilities.

The preacher should try to diagnose the causes of the resistance and to envision different directions the sermon might take to help the congregation release its resistance to the gospel and its promises. Occasionally, the preacher can name the resistance directly and work with the congregation to admit why it resists and to recognize why such resistance is not necessary.

At other times, such an approach would be inflammatory and alienating, and a more indirect approach would be needed. The preacher might begin with a story that raises the subject in a nonthreatening way, or think of an experience that is analogous to the subject but does not immediately cause the congregation to short-circuit.

When facing resistance, a single sermon may not be sufficient. The preacher may need a long-range plan for returning to the subject again and again. The preacher's hopes for the initial sermons may be very modest. In one congregation I know, the pastor wanted to address the subject of homosexuality, but discovered that the mere mention of the subject made listeners uneasy to the point that they could not concentrate on what the preacher was saying. The initial sermons were designed to help the congregation become comfortable with thinking about sexuality.

Draw on Characteristics of How People Learn That Can Enhance the Congregation's Participation with the Subject

In the previous chapter, we reviewed several qualities of learning and teaching, drawn from research into the most effective ways in which people learn. Often the pastor can incorporate these qualities into the sermon to help the listeners participate as fully as possible. The preacher should ask, "Which of these learning modes seem apropos for this sermon? Where, in the sermon, might these qualities come to expression?"

Preachers may find that their own patterns of developing sermons differ from this outline, for pastors, like people in general, develop their own styles of learning. My personality and study habits are such that I ordinarily learn best in a linear fashion, moving methodically from one question or source or subject to the next. I need help to see connections that do not unfold cleanly in linear study, and help to follow hunches that are vague but promising. I am high on the plodding method and low on imagination. But other pastors are more global and associational in their learning. They learn much like one puts together a jigsaw puzzle—a discovery here, a burst of insight there, fervently panting after questions along the way, trial and error. And piece by piece, it comes together.

The important thing is not to follow a particular sequence of steps, but to become cognizant of the way we best encounter subjects on the way to the pulpit, so that we can take advantage of our strengths and compensate for our weaknesses.

CHAPTER • 5

Five Models
for Teaching Sermons

When my spouse and I were co-pastors in Nebraska, an ecumenical agency brought a famous faculty member from a seminary "back east" to lecture on preaching. The lectures were scintillating. The next Monday, I reviewed my extensive notes on the lectures as I began to prepare my sermon, so that I could put the speaker's fresh insights into homiletical practice. The material was still exciting, but I was puzzled about how to translate it into an actual sermon.

So I called around the corner to my spouse's office, "How do I preach this stuff?" As a woman of practical insight, she replied, "Beats me."

This chapter shows how sermons might take actual form as events of teaching and learning. The two previous chapters focused on developing the direction of a teaching sermon and drawing on discoveries in patterns of adult learning to enhance the sermon. We now review five homiletical models which demonstrate ways in which this process of conception and development can result in Sunday preaching. I describe each model, set out its strengths and weaknesses, note occasions when it might be apropos, and offer a sermon to illustrate the model. Each sermon is briefly annotated to explain why the sermon is put together as it is, and what I hope will happen in the listeners as they hear it.

Are these five models the only sermon structures for learning and teaching? Certainly not. The number of possible forms and structures for teaching sermons is limited only by the fact that a preacher will deliver a finite number of sermons in a lifetime. These models are representative of ways that teaching and learning can take practical homiletical form. They can directly suggest the movement for specific sermons, but they may best serve to launch a preacher's own creativity in forming teaching sermons.

Elsewhere, I have called attention to a homiletic model that I consider a staple of the teaching repertoire—a revised version of the Puritan plain sermon.[1] I will not rehash that presentation, except to remind the reader of its simple but highly functional form: (a) Introduction; (b) statement of the subject of the sermon; (c) exegesis of a text or explanation of a topic; (d) theological analysis of the text or topic; (e) application of the discoveries of the analysis of the text or topic to the world of the congregation; (f) conclusion.

My students, who learn this model in class, complain about its woodenness. But after graduation, many report that it has come to their rescue when they have had several good but unfocused ideas for a sermon. The Puritan plain sermon often provides a form on which to structure a satisfactory encounter with a text.

A Model Adapted from Whitehead's Rhythm of Education

The great philosopher Alfred North Whitehead noticed that human beings usually learn in a rhythm that is repeated from one learning experience to another. The rhythm of education consists of three phases which take place as people encounter a subject, engage it, and incorporate it into their patterns of perceiving and acting.[2] These three parts of the cycle of learning can structure a sermon: Romance, Precision, and Generalization. This is an inductive approach to learning and to preaching. The sermon does not make its major point at the beginning. It moves from initial encounter with the subject, through careful study of it, to the major conclusions that are helpful to the congregation.

The Stage of Romance

In this first stage, people become involved with the subject, though they do not usually begin this encounter with a systematic examination of its parts.[3] They begin by noticing the subject and becoming curious about it. For instance, what is it? How do its parts relate to one another? How does it affect those who encounter it? The learner plays with the subject, in the sense of turning it over, examining it, and pondering what it might be able to do or not do. One might think of this stage as similar to the beginning of a romance between two people: fascination, growing magnetism, desire to know more about the other.

In the stage of Romance, the preacher wants the congregation to become interested in the subject. The preacher initiates the sermon by helping the congregation notice aspects of the subject that are intriguing. Is something unusual about it, even surprising? The beginning of the sermon might disclose a glimpse of the subject that suggests promise to the listeners. It might raise questions to which the listeners will want to respond. The pastor hopes the congregation will be lured into wanting to learn more about the subject.

The Stage of Precision

Next, the learner moves from curiosity to comprehension. As the name of the stage implies, the congregation would come to a precise understanding of the subject. The community becomes acquainted with the information, background, questions, and sources that are necessary to have an adequate knowledge of the subject.

When preaching from a biblical text, the preacher wants the congregation to become acquainted with the text in its historical and literary contexts. When preaching from a Christian doctrine, the preacher wants the congregation to be aware of the precise formulation of the doctrine, its biblical roots, and its historic and contemporary manifestations. When preaching on a topic, the preacher wants the congregation to have a clear angle of vision on the topic, and on how the topic has been fathomed (if at all) in other times and places, as well as in the contemporary scene.

The Stage of Generalization

The learner moves beyond the details of interpretation to understand that the subject is important to the meaning of one's own life and to the life of the larger world. From the specifics, the learner discerns patterns that apply to the interpretation of other situations. These can be quite removed from the data that was studied. For example, in a literature class, I study the tragic dimensions of

Macbeth. Later, as I read the story of the downfall of a politician, I think, "A tragedy. Reading *Macbeth* helps me to understand this occurrence." At its best, the generalizing stage results in the formation of a "mental habit." The generalization becomes so thoroughly soaked into my mind that I need not stop and consciously think through each step of interpreting an idea or a situation. I respond according to my ingrained pattern.[4]

The preacher may move from the meanings of a biblical text or doctrine or topic, in its historical or literary circumstances, to the way the material illumines the congregation and its world. Or the preacher might move from a specific situation or question in the contemporary setting to some Christian sources for help in its interpretation, and return to the contemporary setting to reexamine the Christian interpretation of the situation.

This approach to the sermon is suited particularly well to two situations. In the first, the preacher may begin with a biblical text, doctrine, or topic that does not seem especially interesting to the congregation. In the stage of *romance,* the preacher can probe the material for questions, insights, and possibilities that would intrigue the congregation. In *precision* and *generalization,* the preacher would help the people discover the contributions of the text or doctrine to the contemporary life of the church. I suspect that when many contemporary Christians hear that John 14:1-7 ("In my Father's house there are many dwelling places") is the text of the Sunday sermon, they automatically tune to the funeral channel. In the stage of romance, the preacher might pique the congregation's interest by wondering whether this text has any applicability beyond the time of death. And what are these dwelling places, anyway?

In the other situation for which this approach is well suited, the preacher may want to challenge some aspect of the congregation's belief or practice. In *romance,* the preacher could begin by raising questions: "Holy Scripture claims that 'in Christ there is no longer Jew nor Greek, there is no longer slave nor free, there is no longer male and female.' But in this congregation, we are all upper-middle-class Euro-Americans. Does that seem as odd to you as it does to me?" The preacher might then come to a precise understanding that the text, in its Galatian context, describes a Christian community of great variety, in which distinctions have disappeared. The preacher then generalizes to implications for the contemporary congregation.

Sermon: "He Descended into Hell"

This sermon does not center on the exposition of a lone biblical text. It is a topical doctrinal sermon, which both deals with Christ's descent into hell and attempts to model how the church draws upon several important sources in coming to theological clarity.[5]

(Romance) In the romance part of the sermon, I hope the congregation will become intrigued by the subject of the descent of Christ into hell. I try to pique the listeners' curiosity and encourage them to begin to identify their associations with hell.

When was the last time you heard a sermon on hell? I'll bet it's been a long time. The idea of hell does not attract much interest from clergy or congregations in the long-established denominations. It doesn't show up much in our music or liturgies. We do tell jokes that use hell as part of the humor. But I suspect that we hear the term *hell* these days mostly as a part of a mild curse.

Truth to tell, I imagine many people here do not believe in a physical place called hell, where some of the dead suffer. We may have some notion of hell. For instance, I hear people say things such as, "Life is a living hell." But few of the people in my circle of relationships seem to believe in hell as a place of eternal punishment.

So what do we make of this statement tucked away in the Apostles' Creed: "He descended into hell?"[6] What does it mean? Why is it important for us to say it?

(Precision) I move toward understanding how the idea of hell originated and its significance among peoples of antiquity. This information becomes important as I try to identify the surface and deeper dimensions of the notion of hell.

A little background: The idea of hell as a place of punishment for evildoers does not appear strongly in the First Testament. It does mention an abode of the dead called Sheol, but Sheol is not a place of punishment. Many First Testament writers thought of Sheol as a shadowy underworld, where the dead reside without pleasure, without pain, and without the ability to commune with God (e. g., Ps. 88:3-6, 10-12; Ps. 115:17; Job 10:21-22; Isa. 38:18-19; but note Ps. 139:8).

But after most of the First Testament was written, and before Christ, the life of the Jewish people in Palestine became very difficult. Evil came upon them in the form of one oppressive government after another. Many suffered and died.

This situation caused questions to gnaw in the bellies of the Jewish religious leaders. Here is one of the most important questions: How can we say that God is just? How can we say that God does what is right, when the evil people oppress us and prosper, while we languish in captivity and suffering?

The ideas of heaven and hell came about to respond to this ache. Yes, things are unjust in this world, but in the next world, God will do what is right. God will provide a place of everlasting promise and delight for the faithful. But God will consign the wicked to a place of everlasting torture. One of the names for that domicile of pain is *hell*.

Note that hell is not just a place of general suffering. It is designated for the wicked, for those who gave God the Bronx cheer and inflicted suffering on God's people.

Most of the detailed descriptions of hell are found in Jewish documents that are not in the Bible. The pictures that we find in these documents are much like the popular imagination of hell: a place of fire and torment, where people (and evil angels, evil spirits, evil principalities and powers, and the devil) roast throughout the ages.[7]

To be honest, hell is not mentioned very much in the New Testament. But it does come on the screen every once in a while. For instance, in the parable of the sheep and the goats, the great judge consigns the goats to "the eternal fire prepared for the devil and his angels" (Matt. 25:41b). Mark foresees the unfaithful being thrown into hell "where their worm never dies, and the fire is never quenched" (Mark 9:48). In this life, Lazarus' sores were licked by the dogs, but in the next life, he was in Abraham's bosom. In this life, the rich person dressed in purple and fine linen, but in the next life he was in agony in the flames (Luke 16:19-31). And who can forget the lake of fire near the end of the book of Revelation (20:11-15)? And these ideas and images are carried forward by a number of Christian writers elsewhere, after the close of the Bible.

Where, then, do we get the idea that Jesus descended into hell? And what did he do there? I thought I had the answers to these questions in my hip pocket. First Peter says that after Christ was put to death in the flesh, he was "made alive in the spirit, in which also he went and made a proclamation to the spirits in prison" (3:18c-19). Peter also says that "the gospel was proclaimed even to the dead" (4:6).

But the interpretation of the Bible is seldom as easy as you want it to be. When I dug into what biblical scholars have to say about these passages, I found that the spirits in prison are probably fallen angels. Many Jewish people of Peter's day believed that these angels had become superhuman powers who attempted to steal control of the world away from God (e. g., Enoch 67:4–69:1). In the process, they did all manner of evil and generated all manner of pain. According to Peter, the Risen Christ came to them in prison to announce his victory over them. They would have power for a little longer, until the final judgment, but their sun is setting in the sky. And the reference to the gospel being proclaimed to the dead probably refers to Christians who had already died.[8]

Is this all there is to Christ's descent into hell? Christ spits in the eye of the evil spirits? Over the centuries, Christian interpreters have detected more.[9] Some have thought that the phrase refers not to a descent into hell, but into the abode of the dead, a Sheol-like world. This would indicate the depths of Christ's identification with the human condition—between his death on the cross and the resurrection, Christ experienced the fate of every human being. Others have thought that he visited the underworld to offer the possibility of salvation to the righteous who lived prior to Christ.

However, some Christian thinkers recognize something in Jesus' descent into hell that goes beyond anything I have said so far. This thought may not have been intended by Peter, or by the majority of Christian writers through the years. But it is inherent in the logic of God's love. Here it is: The image of Jesus descending into hell is an image of the depth and reach of God's love. Jesus descended into hell to carry God's love to the most disobedient spirits and people. As someone says, "[Love] *hopes all things* (I Cor. 13:7). It (love) cannot do otherwise than hope for the reconciliation of all in Christ. Such unlimited hope is, from the Christian standpoint, not only permitted, but *commanded*."[10] And Catherine of Siena cries out, "If I were wholly inflamed with the fire of divine love, would I not then, with a burning heart, beseech my Creator, the truly merciful One, to show mercy to all?"[11]

But Christians were not the first to hold such sentiments. Centuries before Christ, the psalmist sang:

> Where can I go from your spirit?
> Or where can I flee from your presence?
> If I ascend to heaven, you are there;
> if I make my bed in Sheol, you are there.
> If I take the wings of the morning
> and settle at the farthest limits of the sea,
> even there your hand shall lead me,
> and your right hand shall hold me fast.
> If I say, "Surely the darkness shall cover me,
> and the light around me become night,"
> even the darkness is not dark to you;
> the night is bright as the day,
> for darkness is as light to you.
> Psalm 139:7-12

God seeks us perpetually.

This may be hard for some of us to take. We want people to get what they deserve. Let the punishment fit the crime. It is offensive to think of wicked people getting away unpunished.

Two things: First, the wicked do not get off scott-free. What do you suppose happens as evil people come face to face with the purity of God's love for them in Jesus Christ? I can imagine that they recognize their brutality and sin, and feel a shame that penetrates to the innermost chambers of their hearts. They know they have failed God and that they deserve hell.

I imagine this scenario because I have felt that way before God. Haven't you?

And that leads to the second thing. In God's realm, to my knowledge, there are no degrees of sin. All fall short. Except for the grace of God, we all deserve hell. Why should I begrudge God's generosity to others, when God is already more generous to me than I deserve? If I were in hell this moment, I would be mighty glad to see the elevator open and have Jesus step out and beckon to me.

I take the deep meaning of Jesus' descent into hell to be this: There is no place in the universe that can cut us off from the love of God. Jesus descends into hell for you and for me.

(Generalization) I try now to help the congregation recognize ways in which the deep point of the creed's affirmation of Jesus' descent into hell can affect the congregation's perception and behavior. How does this doctrine affect our thinking about God and our behavior toward other people?

When I think this way about Jesus' descent into hell, it affects my view of God. It makes me even more amazed at God's love, mercy, and compassion. Truly, as the Scriptures say, God is not a mere mortal, who behaves in the heavens in the same way we behave on the earth—tit for tat: You slap me and I'll slap you. You hate me and I'll hate you. Such a God is one who infinitely responds to the worst with the best, who responds to brutality with compassion, who descends into hell and feels its pain—for you and me. And yes, for the people who make my stomach turn.

Jesus' descent into hell also affects my view of other people and my behavior toward them. I don't like to admit this, but I feel superior to a good many people whose moral lives are more degenerate than my own, particularly people who harm themselves and others—drug dealers, abusers, killers. They deserve suffering. I feel sorry for them. But I feel superior. And I keep my distance.

But if Jesus descends into hell for them, then all of us stand on the same ground of grace before God, and in the presence of one another. To be sure, our communities cannot tolerate their evil deeds. And sometimes their evil actions must be restrained forcefully in order to minimize the damage they do to other people and the created order, and even to themselves. But ultimately, I must regard them as persons who are beloved by God. Therefore they deserve my love.

Big question: Does this mean that our actions, thoughts, and feelings don't really count? If God is going to love us in spite of ourselves, why not eat, drink, and be merry? And why not carouse, lie, steal, and kill? If there are no consequences, why bother to have faith or live morally?

But, of course, consequences do befall us when we go against the love and law of God. As Paul said to the Corinthians, "For all who eat and drink without discerning the body, eat and drink judgment against themselves" (I Cor. 11:29). We suffer the consequences of our sin. Children who cheat on the multiplication tables may pass the test. But soon enough, they are in remedial math. And we can make life miserable for others. But when all is said and done, God has the last word. And it is the word of Jesus, descending into hell.

A young man, age sixteen, was at home. His mom was at work for the evening. His mother had told him not to have friends over. But he did. He and his friends should have known not to drink and leave candles unwatched in the basement recreation room.

The boy was burned as he tried to put out the fire. He extinguished the blaze, but he could not extinguish the pain in his body and soul. It was as if he were burning in hell.

The mother could not get home before the ambulance took him to the intensive care unit. She pushed the button beside the door to the unit, and as it swung open, they were face to face across the room.

He could not look at her. He turned his eyes down to the bag collecting urine beside the bed. As she walked across the room, she could feel the pain of his burns. And she could feel the pain in his soul, a hurt no morphine could touch. And she descended into hell.

She reached the bed, put her hand under his chin, and pulled it toward her face. She took him in her arms. And their tears ran together.

There were hard things ahead—hard words, police reports, consequences. But she would be with him. And they would make it.

"Love so amazing, so divine, demands my soul, my life, my all."[12]

The Sermon as Taking a Trip

A learning experience is often like taking a trip.[13] The learners start at a certain point, then move from experience to experience until they arrive at the destination of new insight. Each event, thought, feeling, and discovery along the way adds incrementally to the growing new perspective. The preacher can thus sometimes think of a sermon itself as taking a trip with the congregation. Preacher and congregation start at a given point and journey together through the interstate systems, the state highways and county roads, and even through the alleyways of theological resources, to the debarkation point.

What happens on a trip? Obviously, we get in the car and set out, and we arrive. In between, there are often stops (welcome and unwelcome). What did we forget? Should we go back for it? There may be detours and delays for accidents. The children are interminably asking, "Are we there yet?" The driver suddenly may decide to take a side trip. The map is sometimes reliable, but even recent maps are frequently inaccurate. "I just got this map from AAA, and it does *not* show traffic-stopping construction here!" (fume, fume).

A curve may reveal a beautiful vista not marked on any map. If the road is particularly hilly, the children may need to regurgitate. A breakdown can lead to unexpected help from leftover hippies, driving a Volkswagen van that has been running since 1968. A stop at a gas station turns into an audience with a local philosopher. At last the destination comes into view. We arrive. If we arrive at a place that is new to us, we experience the thrill (or fear or other sense) of exploring its new offerings. Even if we have been to that place before, it may seem different, either because it has changed or because our circumstances or perceptions have changed. Listening to (and preaching) a sermon can be much like taking a trip.

The great strength of this approach is that it follows the pattern of life itself. The sermon is inductive; much of our learning takes place inductively. We do not always begin with a premise from which to draw implications. We often move from discrete observations and experiences to a conclusion, which then serves to orient us in new life experiences.[14] In life, of course, we do not always have a clear sense of where we are going. But along the way, our experiences accumulate, in much the same way the experiences of a journey pile one upon another to create a memory. One of the qualities of a trip that helps make it exciting is the sense of anticipation. What will we see next? What will be waiting for us at the motel tonight? Where will we eat? Now that we are in Nebraska, can we get a buffalo burger? Anticipation is one of the keys to sustaining interest on a trip.[15]

Fred Craddock stresses the importance of pastor and people making the trip together during the sermon: "A preaching event is a sharing in the Word, a trip not just a destination, an arriving at a point for drawing conclusions and not handing over of a conclusion. It is unnatural and unsatisfying to be in a place to which you have not traveled."[16] The preacher does not announce the destination before taking the congregation on the trip.

This model does pose a potential problem for the preacher. The sermon must arrive at a destination that the people can recognize. Sometimes I have heard inductive sermons that appear to have stopped at a breakdown along the side of the road. Furthermore, the sermon must have a sense of movement, of going somewhere, or the congregation is likely to feel it is riding in a car that is circling the parking lot.

Craddock suggests one possible model for a trip—the journey the preacher makes in the encounter with the text, doctrine, or topic.[17] On Monday, the preacher reads the text (or focuses on a doctrine or topic). Questions come up. Issues present themselves for investigation. The preacher does not know where the sermon will end. Throughout the week, the preacher gathers information, thinks about the text in relationship to the congregation, notices connections between the developing sermon, the evening news, and the chatter at the coffee klatch. By the end of the week, a destination is coming into view. For the sermon itself, the preacher could re-create essential aspects of the journey to the main point of the sermon.

Sermon: How Far Christian Unity?

The following sermon is for a congregation of my denomination, the Christian Church (Disciples of Christ). The Disciples have a historic commitment to Christian unity and ecumenical cooperation. The sermon attempts to take the congregation on a journey in which they learn the vision of unity in Ephesians 4:1-6, recall its basis, remember its familiar implications for Christian life, and encounter its wider, perhaps surprising applications. The journey begins with

*the familiar and secure, then moves to the more unfamiliar and
potentially threatening.*

(*Start of the Journey*) Like many of you, I grew up in a congregation of the Christian Church (Disciples of Christ). I loved it. And
one of the things I loved was the slogan we were taught from the
time we could hear: "Christian unity is our polar star." From the
very beginning, our pastors and Sunday school teachers impressed
us with the fact that a part of our church's calling is to witness to
what Christians have in common. Churches have different names,
different practices of baptism, different forms of church government, different ways of partaking of the Lord's Supper, different
titles for their clergy. But beneath the differences, we knew there
was an essential unity.

As I became an adult and talked with people who have joined
our church from other denominations, I notice that our yearning
for unity is one of the most frequent reasons people join us: "We
like the stress on the oneness of the church. We believe in that, too."

(*First Stop*) You can hear this emphasis on the unity of the church
in Ephesians 4. The writer begs the congregation to live a life
worthy of its calling—humility, gentleness, "patience, bearing
with one another in love, making every effort to maintain the unity
of the Spirit in the bond of peace" (Eph. 4:2b-3).

There is something about the way Ephesians points to this vision
that is true to our experience. We long for the unity of the church.
But it is not fully manifest. At present there are divisions in the
church that call for us to regard ourselves with humility and treat
one another with gentleness and love.

This is true also in congregations. Sometimes we cannot even
come to terms with how much to pay the pastor or what color to
paint the closet under the stairs that will be the office for the
Associate Pastor.

There are divisions throughout our denomination. A few years
ago, a sensitive resolution came to the floor of one of our general
assemblies. Emotions ran high. Bible verses were fired back and
forth across the assembly hall like Uzi bullets. An occasional
speaker had a genuine thought. After the vote, you could actually
put your fingers on the pain the room.

There are divisions among denominations. Oh sure, we cooperate on projects such as Week of Compassion, sometimes called One Great Hour of Sharing. Our own denomination is in an ecumenical partnership with the United Church of Christ. In public, everything we say and do is ecumenically correct. But behind the scenes, the gossip and turf wars can make Congressional lobbyists look amateurish.

And there are divisions among different racial and ethnic groups. I wonder how many Euro-American congregations are ready to call an African American as pastor—and vice-versa?

Maintain the unity of the Spirit in the bond of peace—still a timely word.

(*Backtracking*) But why does Ephesians hold this vision? Well, for one thing, the church can be a lot more efficient when it does not have to fight fires in its own sanctuary.

But there is a deeper reason. "There is one body and one Spirit, just as you were called to the one hope of your calling, one Lord, one faith, one baptism, one God and Father of all, who is above all and through all and in all" (Eph. 4:4-6). One! One! One!

Do you hear an echo of this oneness in the First Testament? Yes: "Hear, O Israel: The LORD our God is one LORD (Deut. 6:4 KJV). The oneness of the church mirrors the oneness of God.

Since the unity of the church is rooted in the integrity of God, it is already given. It is not something we achieve through negotiations and votes. Beneath our divisions, God has already made the church one.

We manifest the unity of the church through our actions. As we do, we act out the oneness that is already present. For instance, a few years ago, our general assembly voted to encourage us to adopt a mutual recognition of members and ministers from other denominations. We recognize that United Methodists and Presbyterians and Episcopalians and others are as much Christians and ministers as members of our own denomination. A significant moment! But the achievement of a long negotiating process? No. The vote simply embodied a little of the unity of God's vision for the church.

(*Beautiful Vista*) Now, this idea is beautiful when it involves Christians and churches that are basically similar to us. I've already mentioned the United Church of Christ, Presbyterians, United

Methodists, Episcopalians. We could add the African Methodist Episcopal Church, the African Methodist Episcopal Zion Church, the Christian Methodist Episcopal Church, American Baptists, the Evangelical Lutheran Church in America, the Friends, the Moravians, the Brethren, and others.

We used to think of the Roman Catholics as strange, or even fearful. But today? Sometimes you can hardly tell a Protestant congregation from a Roman Catholic one.

These churches all have minor differences in worship and church government, and in frequency and practice of the Lord's Supper and baptism. But most of us believe pretty much the same things. Some of us publish cooperative Sunday school materials and hold our summer camps jointly. Our children will find it even more difficult than we to distinguish one church from another.

(*Our Old Map Doesn't Show This*) But what about churches that are really different? What about churches that are on the far religious right? What about the sheet-metal tabernacles out on the edge of town, with the garish neon signs, where several of our members have transferred? What about the nationally known television preacher with the slick-backed hair and the limp-backed Bible? What about the Christians in your car pool, who make Rush Limbaugh sound like a pencil-necked liberal geek? And what about churches on the religious left that have meetings in posh hotels, where they discuss the oppressed? And what about the congregation with the newly installed million-dollar pipe organ, where the offering for Week of Compassion (One Great Hour of Sharing) wouldn't buy one skinny cow for hungry people in a developing nation?

I have often felt that I have practically nothing in common with such communities and people except the name *Christian*. In fact, sometimes I am embarrassed to be associated with them under that name.

But if the unity of the church is given in God, then the brute fact is that at a deep level, I am one with them. Not that we all agree on everything, but at a deep level, we are kin, and our differences are among people who share family ties.

(*Side Trip*) I know there are problems with talking about the church as a family.[18] But the text speaks of God as the parent of a family. And the analogy is instructive. In families, people are at different points of development and maturity. There is love, yes, but also rivalry. In the adolescent years, differentiation from parents often leads to mutual frustration. Families can become dysfunctional to the point that family members are healthier when separated (at least while they work out their problems).

But deep down, almost everyone feels a sense of connection. I have always thought that people on my father's side of the family walk with a peculiar gait. Imagine my surprise when I saw a video of myself walking—and plain as day, I could see, for the first time in my life, that same peculiar gait.

When one is wounded, all feel some pain. When one rejoices, all feel some joy. Even family members who are alienated from one another are often curious about the others. And if they are honest, they often would be reconciled, if they could figure out how to attempt reconciliation with minimal risk.

Children who have been adopted into the most loving and satisfying homes often seek to contact their birth parents when they reach adulthood, so deep is the yearning to be connected.

The church is somewhat this way. Different denominations; the religious right and the religious left; the independent Bible congregations and the global Roman Catholic Church—we live in our separate houses, but we have a common parent, and deep in our souls, we are connected.

(*Delay for Theological Repair*) I cannot predict our prospects for reunion, short of the Second Coming. Frankly, it is hard to imagine how we could immediately join our full lives together across the Christian spectrum. But at least we can think of one another as children who are loved unconditionally by the one heavenly Parent (regardless of our theological, political, and social views). We can at least treat one another with the justice that God wills for all.

We can speak to one another and speak of one another with respect. I hear unflattering caricatures of other Christians, and that must stop. It is unjust to represent other people falsely. I confess with shame that I have told jokes—even today from the pulpit—at the expense of televangelists, and that must stop. It is inappropriate in a gospel of unconditional love.

(*Easing out of the Station and onto the Road*) To be sure, we should talk straight with one another. I think it is simply a failure in logic to picket clinics where abortions are performed and to lobby in favor of the death penalty. I am confident that my part of the Christian family has its own failures. Some of the most intolerant people I know are liberals. I have friends in the clergy who can wear out your eardrums with how biblical they are, but who cannot find Zephaniah without using the table of contents.

We must talk honestly and cordially about our differences. But we need to hear one another in our fullness and complexity. We need to find common ground, identify carefully the points of difference, and engage in our ministries without rancor. Most of us will need to take tentative steps in these matters; we do not know how to talk sensitively with other Christians. But our text guides the way when it calls for us to speak in humility and gentleness, and to bear one another in love.

(*Getting Close to the Destination*) If we were reading the whole of Ephesians, we would know that unity of the church is not for its own sake. It is a witness. As the letter says, God's revelation is "set forth in Christ, as a plan for the fullness of time, to gather up all things in him, things in heaven and things on earth" (Eph. 1:9c-10).

Mind-boggling, wouldn't you say? God's ultimate vision is that all things be joined together in one great community, in the same way that God is one. The oneness of the church is designed to testify to the ultimate oneness of all things in God.

A broken church makes only a partial witness, or even a false witness. If we proclaim a gospel of love and justice, but relate to one another with arrogance and injustice, we undercut God's will. If we preach the unity of the church but relate selectively to other Christians, we contradict ourselves.

(*At Last!*) But when the oneness of the church comes into view, it makes a powerful witness. In the late 1980s, the small community of Manchester, Indiana, decided to form a committee to resolve some local conflicts. Barry and Cliff were two leading members. Barry had received the Purple Heart in Vietnam. Cliff was a conscientious objector who continues to protest militarism by keeping their income below the taxable level and refusing to pay the phone bill's federal excise tax, which pays for military expenditures. The two men were wary of each other.

But during a drive to a meeting, they discovered that they had parallel experiences. Barry had gone to Vietnam at the call of his government and tried to do his best. When he returned, he "discovered that he was an alien." He felt unsupported, that he "had done a dirty job for the United States and then was rejected when he came back."[19]

Cliff said, "Being a conscientious objector pushes a person into the same feeling of alienation, of being a sort of outcast from society. I had felt on the edge, not only of society but also of the church [the Church of the Brethren] in which I had been nurtured."[20]

Today, the two continue to get together. Barry goes out to Cliff's place. "Sometimes we'll sit on the porch and talk for a couple of hours."

When the war between the United States and Iraq began, Barry said, "You and I will never agree on the war in Vietnam, but on an issue that is as clear as this . . . clearly a war to defend our materialism, where's the Church of the Brethren?"

Cliff responds, "His words were an impetus to get me on the stick."[21]

The oneness of the church brings us together in surprising ways. It is a gift from God to a broken world. I want to find ways to witness to that unity. Don't you?

A Socratic Sermon Model

In popular memory, Socrates is recalled as one who taught by asking questions. In this light, the sermon can become a series of questions and responses which move toward discernment. In *Design for Preaching*, H. Grady Davis calls this method "a question propounded." He says of it, "This form is distinguished from all others in that its essence is not assertion but inquiry."[22]

The questions that form the basis of the sermon must be real questions in which the congregation has some stake. They cannot be merely rhetorical devices to attract listener attention. "If the question is just an excuse for telling the answer, the idea's form is assertion, not question."[23]

A real question creates cognitive dissonance in the listeners, as we noted in chapter 3. A question can crack open a window in the listeners' worldviews and encourage them to reflect on the adequacy of those views.

The best questions are ones in which the listeners can hear their own queries of God, the Bible, doctrine, ethics, and life. They create a degree of cognitive dissonance in the hearer, as we saw in chapter 3. In the sermon that follows, I am able to cite questions that have come from the listeners themselves.

Of course, the sermon moves as far as possible toward resolving the questions raised. Usually, the preacher will be able to respond fully. But some issues are complicated; insight and revelation are dim. At such times, the preacher may answer only in part. Or the preacher may answer for herself or himself and allow the listeners to do the same. On rare occasions, particularly during seasons of lamentation, it may be enough simply to ask the question and lay it before the congregation and God.

When preaching in this mode, the preacher's most important task is to distinguish questions that are fundamental from those that are secondary. The following illustrates how a series of questions might form the structure of a sermon:

1. What is the major question that surfaces from the text, the doctrine, or the topic?

2. What is at stake for the Christian community in this subject?

3. From what does this question arise? (Is it a theological problem? A cultural issue? A moral question?)

4. What resources can help us converse with this question and its issues? (For example, the Bible? Voices from Christian tradition? Our experience with the subject? The social sciences? The arts? Contemporary theology?)

5. What are some different possibilities for responding to the question or resolving the issue?

6. What are the strengths and weaknesses of these resolutions? Which seem more or less appropriate to the gospel, more or less intelligible, more or less plausible?

7. What, then, shall we conclude?

8. What are the implications of this conclusion for the thoughts, feelings, and actions of the congregation?

Of course, different subjects will often result in different structures for the sermon.

Socratic preaching is especially suited to subjects about which the congregation is unsettled—unresolved matters of faith, doctrine, and moral behavior. The questioning format allows the congregation to be introduced to enlarged patterns of thought without feeling confronted or attacked. The questioning mode also models how to think through a text or an issue. At the same time, the questions that are asked model for the congregation how to ask questions of important subjects. The listeners may make the jump from the questions the preacher asked of one subject to the questions they can ask of other subjects. However, the preacher who uses this approach needs to be careful not to ask so many questions that the congregation is overwhelmed.

Sermon: Come, Sophia.

In 1993, an international ecumenical conference of 2,000 women in Minneapolis, called Re-imagining, set off firestorms in many congregations. One of the points of combustion was the conference's use of the term Sophia as a way of speaking of the Holy. Many of those who reacted against the conference charged that the term introduced goddess worship into the Christian community. Some laypeople immediately assumed that the charges were true and became quite energized, even hostile. Many, perhaps most, were filled with questions. They were not hostile, but genuinely concerned. Some in the congregations applauded the conference.

The following is a teaching sermon that might be preached in such a controversial setting.[24] The beginning of the sermon attempts to help the congregation recognize its own questions and relationship to the topic. The preacher uses a series of questions to structure the sermon and help the congregation keep its mind open. I ask the congregation to put its resistance on hold, in order to keep an open mind during the sermon.

I begin with a question. When you are making an important decision, what do you like to have? I'll bet you like to have as much information as you can about the subject. The basic info, the positives, the negatives, and as much as you can handle in between.

Your questions around the church, and your phone calls, and even a couple of letters, have let me know that many of you are concerned about the reports that have come from the conference on Re-Imagining. This was a conference of about 2,000 people, mostly women, held last fall in Minneapolis. Its purpose was to offer women an opportunity to envision what the church might be like in the future.

Along the way, the conference used the term *Sophia*. As a preacher came to the lectern, the members of the conference would pray for Sophia to bless and empower the speaker. Most of your questions have centered around the use of this term. Here are some of the questions: Where did the word *Sophia* originate? What does it mean? Why was it used at a Christian meeting? And the question that seemed to generate the most energy: Did the conference engage in goddess worship when it invoked *Sophia?*

Now, some of your emotions are high on this topic. Some are very affirmative. Many are curious. A few are hostile. But I know you well enough to know that all of you want to be fair. When it comes to making a major decision, you like to have all the information in front of you. So this morning, I ask everyone to set your emotions and preconceptions on low and listen to the information and perspectives in the sermon.

After the service, the deacons have scheduled a conversation hour in the parlor, so that we can explore some of these matters in more detail. We will have plenty of opportunity for question and answer, give and take.

Your own question is a good starting point. *Where did the term Sophia originate?* Sophia is a Greek word, a feminine noun that means "wisdom." If you know someone named Sophie, you know someone named Wisdom. The Jewish people used the term *sophia* to translate their Hebrew word *hokma,* also a feminine noun for "wisdom." This is biblical language. We find the word *hokma* in the First Testament and the word *sophia* in the New.

So, what is wisdom in the Bible? Wisdom is the quality of being able to discern God and God's ways from those forces and ways that are not of God. The opposite of wisdom is folly—being unwilling to recognize the divine will and purpose. The Bible often contrasts wisdom and folly. For example: "The wise are cautious and turn away from evil, but the fool throws off restraint and is careless" (Prov. 14:16).

For our study this morning, I call attention to a very important development. Wisdom is more than a quality of human understanding. Some of the writers of the Hebrew Scriptures speak of wisdom as if it is a person: "Wisdom cries out in the street; in the squares she raises her voice" (Prov. 1:20).

In this mode, wisdom is an agent or representative of God. Wisdom mediates God's presence and purposes in the world.

God created wisdom before the world was created. In Proverbs, wisdom says, "Ages ago, I was set up, at first, before the beginning of the earth" (8:23). And not only that, but wisdom helped to fashion the world: "When [the LORD] established the heavens, I was there . . . . I was beside him, like a master worker; and I was daily his delight" (Prov. 8:27, 30).

This is important stuff. And it gets more impressive. The Jewish people in the ancient world wrote a number of books that are not included in most of our Protestant Bibles. Some of these contain ideas that are important to our investigation of wisdom. They are also important to understanding parts of the New Testament.

A book called Ecclesiasticus (or Sirach or Ben Sira) declares, "One alone is wise, the Lord most terrible, seated upon [the] throne" (1:8 REB). But God is so closely identified with wisdom that this writer can say, "To serve her [wisdom] is to serve the Holy One, and the Lord loves those who love her" (4:14 REB).[25] And Ecclesiasticus goes to great lengths to point out that God lavishes wisdom upon all the living, on Jewish and Gentile people alike (1:10).

Another book, the Wisdom of Solomon, is even more emphatic. The writer says that wisdom is "intelligent, holy, unique, manifold, subtle, mobile, clear, unpolluted . . . loving the good, keen, irresistible, beneficent . . . all powerful, overseeing all" (7:22-23). "Like a fine mist she rises from the power of God, a clear effluence from the glory of the Almighty . . . . She is the radiance that streams from everlasting light, the flawless mirror of the active power of God, and the image of [God's] goodness. She is but one, yet can do all things" (Wisdom of Solomon 7:25-27*a* REB).

Let us be clear. Wisdom is not God. But she is in as close a proximity to God as any created thing can be.

Is wisdom found only in the Hebrew Bible and in the writings of the Jewish people? No. Not surprisingly, several of the earliest Christian writers use terminology drawn from the wisdom tradition to help interpret the significance of Jesus Christ. At the beginning of First

Corinthians, Paul describes the content of his preaching: "We proclaim Christ crucified . . . Christ the power of God and the *wisdom* of God" (1:23-24). The letter of Colossians quotes an ancient hymn: "[Christ] is the *image* of the invisible God, the firstborn of all creation; for in him all things in heaven and on earth were created" (1:15). We hear the same language in the Gospel of John: "All things came into being through him" (1:3). And when Jesus says, "Come to me, all you that are weary. . . . Take my yoke upon you" (Matt. 11:28), he echoes wisdom talk from Ecclesiasticus: "Come to her [wisdom]. . . . Her yoke is a golden ornament" (6:19, 30 REB; cf. 24:19). God is present in the world through Christ, much like God is present through wisdom. By understanding the background of wisdom in the Old Testament, we can understand God's revelation through Christ.

Is Sophia, wisdom, a pagan goddess? I hope that by this point, the answer is clear. In the Bible, *Sophia* is not God. She is an agent of God. She helped create the world. She mediates God's presence and purposes. Her function in the Hebrew Bible helps us to understand how Christ functions.

A little nuancing is required here. In the Bible, *Sophia* is not a name for God.[26] However, some Christian thinkers today use *Sophia* as an expression for the divine self and for Christ. To be candid, when they do this, they go beyond the Bible. I am not ready to make that move myself. But I can understand why it is important for some people to do so. I do not regard it as heresy for others to speak of God with the name of *Sophia,* and I cannot understand how the church could regard it as heresy. In any case, every generation has added names to the vocabulary with which we speak of God; the name *Sophia* has some precedent in sacred scripture.

Why did Sophia make her way into a Christian meeting? Through the centuries, most of the language and symbols of the Christian faith have been masculine. Even the term *Lord* was originally a masculine term (and still denotes masculinity to many people). Now, a number of expressions for God in the Bible and in Christian tradition are feminine or have no gender reference. But a high percentage of our language for God has drawn on male associations— Father, King, Master. And Jesus was a male. These associations combine to minimize the awareness of women and their experience in the Christian community. Many have felt left out, even downgraded or oppressed. And when the church's vocabulary in reference to God is largely masculine, the Christian community is not able to draw fully on feminine worlds in order to interpret the Christian faith.

Sophia is a biblical expression that brings the experience of women into the heart of Christian faith. Women can resonate with Sophia. As a woman said to me once, "When I hear the word *Sophia*, I know intuitively, in the depths of my being, that God understands me. I know that God feels what I feel. My experience can be a window to reveal the divine life to me, to other women, to men." *Sophia* helps women be aware of the divine presence.

God, of course, is neither male nor female. God transcends gender. Indeed, God transcends all our capacities to speak fully about the divine self. When we speak about God, we use the language of realities and relationships that help us understand aspects of the divine life. *Sophia* can help us appreciate how women's lives can deepen our understanding of God.

I was born with a large birthmark on my forehead. A skin graft covered it when I was six months old, but when I was a child, the skin graft was still quite noticeable. Other children would ask, "What's wrong with your head?" Even adults would stoop and stare.

When I was about eight, I was with some neighborhood kids. We were building a dam across a drainage ditch down the block. A new kid came up, looked me full in the face, and cried out, "That's the ugliest thing I've ever seen."

I was crushed. I climbed out of the ditch and ran home into the kitchen, where my mother wrapped my sobbing body in her apron. She was there. For me. She mediated God's presence. For me. That day, I called her Mother. Today, I might call her *Sophia*.

I imagine we all have similar moments. The Bible helps us to know what they are: the wisdom that makes God known to us.

The Sermon As Jigsaw Puzzle

Learning sometimes takes place in a linear fashion. Discovery and insight logically follow discovery and insight. Most curriculum in public school, college, and seminary assumes this pattern. However, much learning is more random. The learner picks up some information here, a question there, a fact along the way. Gradually, a framework for understanding emerges.

The latter process may be compared to putting together a jigsaw puzzle.[27] The pieces of the puzzle are available on the table top. But they are in disarray. None are connected. Some are sideways and upside down. Some are at the opposite end of the table from their location in the finished picture. You pick one up and turn it over and over, trying to figure out where it fits. A few pieces go together, and after awhile the outline of the picture begins to emerge. With patience and direction, the picture comes into focus, and you know where to put more and more of the pieces. The jigsaw puzzle makes use of associative learning, rather than linear learning.

This can serve as a model for the way a teaching sermon comes together. The preacher takes individual pieces of the puzzle and turns them over. What do these mean? To what larger picture can they point? Gradually, the individual pieces begin to form a larger picture.

The jigsaw puzzle is an especially useful model for sermons on detailed biblical texts. The preacher needs to discuss many of these details, but they do not fit together in a neat sequence. The preacher can discuss each image and gradually bring the images into relationship with one another, to help the congregation perceive the meaning(s) of the whole passage. For instance, this would be a good way to preach from the apocalyptic visions of Mark 13, Matthew 24, or Luke 21.

The jigsaw puzzle pattern also would be useful when a sermon needs to bring together different kinds of data, in order to come to theological clarity about a biblical text, a Christian doctrine, or an issue of faith or ethics. For instance, when a congregation needs to consider whether abortion is a possible Christian option, the jigsaw puzzle might provide a format to bring together data from the Bible, from the tradition, from the experience of women and men who have chosen (and who have not chosen) the path of abortion, and from norms generated by contemporary theology.

Also, the jigsaw puzzle could structure a sermon whose text or topic is intriguing, but when its relationship to the congregation is not immediately clear. The preacher could consider the fascinating qualities of individual parts of the scene, so as to touch the nerve of congregational interest. For example, the jigsaw puzzle might serve a sermon in which the preacher ponders the possible implications of a new scientific discovery.

The jigsaw puzzle format does have its dangers. It is easy for the preacher to flood the sermon with pieces of data that remain isolated, leaving the congregation confused. "Well, we heard a lot of interesting stuff, but when the sermon was finished, I couldn't make heads or tails of it." The pastor may find it difficult to help the congregation sense that the sermon is moving toward a goal. When preaching in this genre, it is essential for the pieces to fit together, so that the congregation has the sense that a larger picture (and one worth seeing) is actually in the future.

Sermon: The Temple at Seventh and Delaware (I Kings 8:22-54)

This sermon was preached at the 100th anniversary of the dedication of the building for Central Christian Church in Indianapolis. I hoped that the congregation would name (or rediscover) the ways in which their building communicates a sense of the holy. For this purpose, I used Solomon's temple as a paradigm for how architectural space can evoke awareness of the divine presence.[28] I also hoped the congregation would learn some basic information about the temple at Jerusalem.

(*Putting the Border of the Puzzle in Place*) What is the longest prayer you can remember? Maybe it was Thanksgiving Day when you were eight years old. It was warm, as Thanksgivings go, and you had been running around outside all morning. When your parents called you for the big dinner, you were so hungry your stomach was tied up in knots. Uncle Frank prayed. Uncle Frank thanked God for every item of creation and every relative you ever had in your family tree. And then he thanked God for every piece of turkey; he prayed for each piece separately. By the end of the prayer, the lunch hour had passed, and it was almost time for supper.

The prayer from First Kings that I read a few moments ago (Solomon's prayer of dedication for the temple), falls into the category of long prayers. In fact, for length, it may be an Olympic gold-medal winner.

But Solomon had good reason for praying such a long prayer. The people of Israel had just completed their temple. And they were overflowing with thanksgiving to God. They were probably much like the crowd that filled this sanctuary when this building was dedicated, exactly 100 years ago.

I wish I had a projector and screen to show slides of Solomon's temple. The temple courts were not quite the size of a football field. The whole area was walled with white stone. And the wall was a little higher than the fence between the houses on "Home Improvement," where Tim the Tool Man and Wilson the Neighbor have their conversations. The temple building itself was in the middle of the court. And it was about the size of this sanctuary.

(*First Piece*) Two giant pillars stood at the entrance to the temple. They were named Jachin and Boaz. From Hebrew, those names could be roughly translated, "God establishès" and "[God] comes with power." The presence of the pillars was a signal that God was in residence in the temple.

You don't have giant pillars outside your sanctuary door, but you do have a great tower. And I'll bet that as you pass into this solid brick building, you have the sense that something solid is here. Just think of the difference between walking into Central Christian Church and walking into Sleaze-Bag Discount Store. When I enter this building, I have the sense that this is *Some Place!* And in this transient cinder-block world, we need places that orient us.

(*Second Piece*) Off to one side of the temple was a giant basin that held 12,000 gallons of water. They called it the molten sea. But it was not an indoor swimming pool. In the ancient world, many people believed that water had three meanings.

1. It was for cleansing. People who saw the molten sea remembered the cleansing power of God.

2. Water was the source of fertility. No water: no crops, no life in the winter. So the presence of the molten sea reminded the community that God faithfully provided for their needs.

3. Many in antiquity also thought that water was a power of chaos. Just this week, underground Chicago has been flooded. Just ask those people if they can understand water as chaos. But in the molten sea, the water was calm. The worshipers who beheld the molten sea were reminded that no matter how powerful the chaos, God has the more powerful word and would one day calm the chaos.

How about it? Do you know people who feel that chaos is trying to pull them into its undertow today? Somalia. Bosnia. On the streets nearby. One of our sons and I took our congregation's turn in the child-care center, at the shelter for the homeless just up the street.

As the evening was winding down, one of the children, about four years old, came up to us and said, "Do you have a house? Can I go home with you?" Oh.

I don't know that these stained-glass windows and this walnut paneling and those masonry pillars are quite like the molten sea. But I'll bet that if your life were in chaos, and you came in here, you could feel something bigger than you are, something firm and undergirding, something that can hold you against the undertow.

(*Third Piece*) The altar of sacrifice was nearby, and it was often dripping with blood from the animals that had been sacrificed. Sometimes we Christians are critical of the practice of sacrifice. Some of us are even repulsed by it. And many of us are blood-phobic, especially because of the diseases carried by the blood today. But the point of sacrifice is really very simple. Sacrifice was to assure the congregation that it was accepted by the awesome, holy God who dwelt in the awesome temple.[29]

Blood was a symbol of life. The people making a sacrifice would lay their hands on the animal, signifying that the blood of the animal stood for them. Then the animal would be killed (in a quick and relatively painless procedure). They would place the blood on the altar as a symbol that the Great Lifegiver accepted them, loved them, and would be faithful to them.

I wonder sometimes if we should have something like that altar in our churches—a place where we could take a drop of our own blood and see it symbolically received by the living God. Aren't there times in your life when you feel inadequate, unclean, sinful? And wouldn't you like to have a concrete demonstration that your life, and all your pitiful feelings and actions, are held in the heart of God? But then, what do we have here? The Lord's Table. A chalice. And what is it that we say? "This is my blood, poured out for you."

(*Fourth Piece*) And in the center of the temple was the Holy of Holies, a cube about six feet on each side. No windows. Completely dark. In its center, the ark of the covenant. And over the ark, two cherubim, angel-like figures with outstretched wings. The people believed that in the space between the wings and the ark, God dwelled. That is what the Bible means when it says that God dwells in thick darkness.

Like a summer night, when the fever of the day is cooled, and you lie in your backyard or on your balcony or on your roof or in the park. And something is there—something good, something right, something for you. You can't see it. But you can feel it. And you can almost touch it.

Does that ever happen in this room? I know it has in the past. When I was growing up in a small town in Missouri (a town about the size of your choir loft), going to a funeral was a main event. And during my childhood years, one of the favorite songs for funerals in our town was "Beautiful Isle of Somewhere."

> Somewhere the sun is shining,
> Somewhere the song-birds dwell.
> Hush, then, thy sad repining;
> God lives, and all is well.
> Somewhere, Somewhere,
> Beautiful Isle of Somewhere!
> Land of the true, where we live anew—
> Beautiful Isle of Somewhere![30]

Now, today that might not be everything you want in a Christian song. But it brought a moment of hope to families and friends whose hearts had shriveled up in their chests. And it was written by Jessie Brown Pounds, a woman who was a member of Central Christian Church. She wrote it one Sunday when an ice storm prevented her from going to worship. "Somewhere the sun is shining"—even if not in Indianapolis.

Can you imagine that? Someone came alive to the presence of God in this very room, and wrote a song that touched people all across this continent.

You can't always see these things happening, of course. Zerelda Wallace brought her son, Lew Wallace, to Sunday school here. According to the church record, he was a "passive student." That is a delicate way to put it—passive. But when he was at the height of his powers, he wrote *Ben Hur*, subtitled: *A Tale of the Christ*. The other night, our family rented the video of that movie. Two cassettes—just right for a long summer night when everyone is hot and tired and cranky. And I must admit that our children were more interested in the chariot race than in the Christ. But who knows? Who knows what is getting across today, because of what happened here to a young member who was called "passive"? And who can imagine what might be happening in your hearts and minds even now?

(Fifth Piece) So, no wonder Solomon prays this long prayer. There is much for which to be thankful. "O LORD, God of Israel, there is no God like you in heaven above or on earth beneath, keeping covenant and steadfast love for your servants who walk before you with all their heart" (I Kings 8:23). And the prayer goes on and on, blessing God for unfathomable and inexhaustible goodness.

(Sixth Piece) But in the midst of this prayer, did you notice something striking? Solomon specifically prays for God to be responsive to foreigners: "Hear in heaven your dwelling place, and do according to all that the foreigner calls to you, so that all the people of the earth may know your name . . . as do your people Israel" (I Kings 8:43).

Who is the foreigner today? I am not exactly a world traveler, but three years ago, our family spent the summer in Zambia, a nation in Africa. And we were sometimes the only Caucasian people for miles. We traveled to villages and huts in the bush that are utterly premodern. A woman's only possession might be a cooking pot and a piece of cloth, to use as a bed at night and a dress in the daytime.

But in Zambia, I never felt I was in a strange land as much as I do on some street corners in Indianapolis. Or when I turn on the radio and hear certain talk-show hosts say things that seem utterly outside the realm of the possible. I know I am in a foreign land when they are the best of the listening spectrum. And even in church, I sometimes hold my breath, wondering, "How can a Christian say such a thing?"

Yet, the God of the temple is their God, too. I may not agree with them. I may think they misunderstand and misrepresent God. But at the deepest level, I must believe that God wills good for them, too. And God takes every opportunity to lead them (and you and me) into larger visions of truth.

And anyway, when it comes to deserving a reserved seat in the temple, aren't we all foreigners?

(*Looking at the Whole Picture*) I've been going on about what a great place the temple was and what a wonderful place this is. But did you notice what Solomon prayed? "Even heaven and the highest heaven cannot contain you, much less this house that I have built" (I Kings 8:27*b*).

What we experience of God here, in the temple, is a microcosm of what God offers us everywhere. The way God is with us in this sacred place is the way God is with us in every place.

If you are like me, you forget that from time to time. When I am having a fight with a colleague and my classes are as exciting as rocks gathering moss on the bottom of the White River, and I've got a stack of papers to read as high as the ceiling in this sanctuary, and I go home and I'm in a second-floor bedroom, where the windows are painted shut and I'm trying to change a world-class diaper, it is easy to forget that there's anything more in this universe.

That's why we need a temple. That's why God gives us a beautiful place like this. That's why God gives us people like you. So that brick and stone and flesh can remind us that the God who lives in the temple at Seventh and Delaware is the God who lives in the temple at your house, and in your heart.

A Sermon Structure Adapted from Paul Ricoeur's Model

Paul Ricoeur, one of the giants of contemporary hermeneutics, proposes a model of engaging a text that can easily serve as a pattern for a teaching sermon. Ricoeur's approach can be applied to the interpretation of biblical texts and Christian doctrines as they have developed through history, as well as to contemporary questions, situations, and issues. Ricoeur contends that mature, critical interpretation moves through three stages.[31]

First Naiveté

The initial stage is called First Naiveté. In this phase, the reader enters a text at a precritical level. The reader assumes the adequacy and truthfulness of the passage.

In First Naiveté, which would constitute the first part of the sermon, the preacher might simply describe the way in which a congregation has viewed a text, a doctrine, or an issue. At this juncture, the preacher would not challenge that view, but would attempt, as carefully and fully as possible, to help the congregation recognize its perception.

Critical Reflection

The second stage is critical consciousness or critical reflection. In this stage, the interpreter questions two things: (1) The degree to which the worldview (or ideology) of the text is controlled by hidden assumptions that serve to support certain persons, values, and practices (and downgrade others); (2) The degree to which interpreters are influenced by their own assumptions that support certain persons, values, and practices (and downgrade others).

The assumption behind the need for critical reflection is that texts (and doctrines, situations, and interpreters) are often biased in their approach to the world. They frequently assume that certain people, values, and practices are normative. Often these qualities lift up selected people, institutions, and practices, while diminishing or oppressing others. As long as these factors remain unexamined, they exert power and control in the act of interpretation. The reader is unaware of the vested interests that are being promoted and denied.

Ricoeur, followed by most contemporary scholars of hermeneutics, contends that the reader must unmask these often unrecognized factors. The factors can be related to psychology, sociological situation, economic preservation, political power, gender, race, theology. In Ricoeur's famous phrase, the interpreter engages in a "hermeneutics of suspicion" in the phase of critical reflection.[32] Preachers should be suspicious of both the assumptions of the text and their own assumptions. Whose vested interests are upheld by the text or the preacher's worldview? Whose interests are denied? Does the promise of a text seem too good to be true?

Liberation theologians have been among the most forceful (in the Christian community) to call attention to the importance of the hermeneutics of suspicion. At the level of First Naiveté, Christians (and persons of other religions) tend to use religious traditions, texts, values, and practices to justify their own worldviews and lifestyles.

In the phase of critical reflection, the preacher would try to help the congregation gain critical perspective on the text. The preacher needs to identify the issues which the congregation most needs to engage in the mode of critical reflection. These often include the distance in culture and values between the world of the Bible and the congregation's world. They also include assumptions about the roles and places of people and practices in the community.

One of the best ways to prompt such reflection is to raise questions about the adequacy of the congregation's understanding of the text, doctrine, issue, or situation. Another useful strategy is to introduce data (e. g., texts, stories, situations, viewpoints of recognized authorities) into the sermon that are dissonant with the First Naiveté. I try to take advantage of both these possibilities in the sermon that follows.

Second Naiveté

Ricoeur calls the third phase of the hermeneutical movement the Second Naiveté. The interpreter now returns to the text and receives it as informed by critical consciousness. The interpreter is aware of the many problems inherent within the text (and within the interpreter). But the readers are now able to draw out those aspects of the text (and of the interpreter's own consciousness and life situation) that can be of abiding value.

In this third moment of the sermon, Second Naiveté, the preacher returns to the text informed by critical consciousness. The pastor attempts to help the congregation either draw out of the text those qualities that are of continuing importance or to recognize alternative ways of understanding the issues posed by the text.

Of course, the preacher never reaches a pure conclusion. Interpretation is always colored (and discolored) by the worldview and context of the text and the interpreting community. Every interpretation is precisely that: an *interpretation*. The material in critical reflection, and in the Second Naiveté, should themselves be subjected to further critical reflection. However, the preacher aims to become as conscious as possible of the factors that enhance and warp our reading of a text. Preachers offer their best insights against the background of their circumstances at a given time, recognizing that more light may yet break forth.

This model for a sermon would be great help when the pastor has identified a biblical passage, a doctrine, or a congregational practice or assumption that needs to be challenged. First Naiveté would allow the community to enter the sermon in a friendly and secure environment. In Critical Reflection, the congregation would reconsider its understanding. Second Naiveté encourages the congregation to leave the sermon with a strong, positive, mature understanding of the way the text can benefit them in the future.

However, a warning sign should be posted in the preacher's consciousness when working on the phase of critical reflection. The hermeneutics of suspicion are essential. But it is easy to let the discoveries that emerge from suspicion become the most prominent features of the sermon. To be candid, the bad news that emerges from the hermeneutic of suspicion is often more dramatic than the good news that comes in the Second Naiveté.

This is particularly true when the preacher discovers that pain, abuse, and suffering may result from a biblical text or a Christian doctrine or practice. The preacher can easily dig such a deep hole that the congregation is unable to climb out; the listeners become so depressed (or angry) by the indictment that they are not able to receive the good news of the Second Naiveté.

Studies of adult learners show that a positive vision is by far the most compelling reason for learners to adopt new viewpoints. While the preacher does not want to downplay the results of critical analysis, it is crucial that the future vision be more emotionally and intellectually compelling than the results of the hermeneutic of suspicion. Otherwise, the congregation may be immobilized by guilt (or frustration).

Sermon: "What Kind of Shepherd Is God?" (Psalm 23)

In this sermon, I hope the congregation will learn (or re-learn) some important information about Psalm 23 that will help them move from a surface to a deeper understanding of God as shepherd. I also hope that the congregation will experience God's shepherding care through the medium of the sermon. Along the way, I hope that the sermon encourages the congregation to see the importance of critically examining the traditional interpretations of biblical texts and Christian beliefs.

(First Naiveté) Psalm 23 is familiar. In the first part of the sermon, I try to help the listeners recall their familiar associations with the passage. I hope they will feel that God is a tender and compassionate shepherd.

"The Lord is my shepherd, I shall not want." This passage is one of the most loved in the Bible. While preparing this sermon, I went through the notes I have kept from the funeral services that took place while I was a pastor in a congregation. At the request of the families, we used this psalm for more than 75 percent of the services. And no wonder. The Twenty-third Psalm echoes a deep sense of God's love for each of us.

When I spent a summer in Israel working at an archaeological site, a shepherd came by almost daily with a large flock of sheep.[33] Strong. Muscular. Clad in a rough woven garment. Swarthy skin. Deep-set brown eyes. Powerful but gentle.

Now, a sheep looks like a generic sheep to me. But he could call each one by name, and they would come to him. The shepherd lives with the sheep in the field. Day and night. Summer and winter. Always with them.

We were in Israel in the drought of summer. The fields were so dry that the stubble from the harvest cracked underfoot like sticks popping. But just as the psalm says, the shepherd knew where to find springs and little patches of green grass. Incidentally, the sheep need still, quiet water, because they have a hard time drinking from tumbling streams.

And the shepherd knew how to prepare the pasture. The digestion of sheep is easily upset by noxious weeds, and they can cut their faces in briars. So the shepherd would pull the weeds and trim the briars before allowing the sheep to enter a pasture.

The shepherd knew how to get from one place to another. Sheep cannot see well, so they can easily let a leg slip into a crevice. Snap—the leg is broken. So the shepherd knows smooth paths from one pasture to another.

And when a sheep cuts its face, the shepherd anoints it with medicine to help the cut heal. Can you feel those gentle, strong hands on your face, tenderly applying balm to a cut?

The psalm assures us that God is like a shepherd. Ever with us. Knowing each of us by name. Doing all that God can do to strengthen us. With us in pain and sorrow.

Not long ago, I visited with a woman whose husband of forty-three years had died. This is what she said to me:

> When I stood there at the casket, it felt like my heart had been pulled out of my chest. For the longest time, I couldn't get to sleep at night. I'd lie there and hear the clock chime. What a hollow sound. Chiming up the stairs of the empty house. One. Two. Three. Then I started to say the Twenty-third Psalm. At first I'd say it dozens of times. But now, I only say it a few times, and then next thing I know, it's morning. And I feel better. When I say the words, I feel God with me.

(Critical Reflection) In this part of the sermon, I try to help the congregation think critically about the image of God as shepherd. In particular, I encourage the listeners to reflect on the fact that in the world of the Bible, the shepherd was more than a tender caregiver. Sometimes the shepherd had to say "No." I also hope that they will reflect on the apparent discrepancy between some of the affirmations of the psalm (for example, "I shall not want") and the experience of people for whom those affirmations do not appear to be true.

However, for all its beauty, there are some surprising and bothersome things about this psalm. "Thy rod and thy staff, they comfort me." The rod is a club the shepherd uses to beat off robbers. The staff is much like a shepherd's crook that you see in pictures. The shepherd uses the staff for a lot of things, and among them is discipline. Sometimes the shepherd must tell the sheep "No." And if the sheep do not respond to the verbal command, the shepherd may set the staff directly in front of them, like a fence post. Or if a sheep is particularly recalcitrant, the shepherd may give it a whack. Is this the kind of comfort you want from your shepherd? A whack?

This raises another problem with the psalm. When we compare God to a shepherd, we compare ourselves to sheep—not a flattering comparison. Here are five qualities of sheep:

1. They have poor eyesight and can only see a few feet;
2. Consequently, they tend to follow one another around;
3. They are cranky; they bite one another inordinately;
4. They have delicate digestive systems and easily get indigestion;
5. They are not known for their intelligence. They require a lot of care to survive.[34]

I find the comparison somewhat offensive. What about you?

But the psalm raises an even tougher question. God is my shepherd. Yes. "I shall not want." God "makes me lie down in green pastures." But the brute fact is that these promises do not always come true.

We do want. Our pastures are not always green. As I touch up this sermon for use in this book, monumental floods in south Georgia cover the pastures, the roads, the towns, the houses, the hospitals. Lifetimes of memories are washed away in a few moments. More than a million people are streaming from their homes in Rwanda, a land torn by civil war, into Zaire. Zaire itself has been a bloody nation these last ten years. And I'll bet every person here knows someone dying a long and excruciating death from cancer or HIV/AIDS. Can you stand at the beside of someone withering from AIDS and look them in their hollow eyes and recite these words?

(Second Naiveté) In this section of the sermon, I try to help the congregation return to the text at a deeper level. I want the congregation to become aware that God's care is most fully expressed when it includes discipline (helping people to recognize their weaknesses, problems, and sin, and take responsibility for them). And I hope the listeners will understand that while God cannot prevent difficulty, God's presence can shepherd them through difficulty.

But you know, when I come back to this passage at a deeper level, I realize that it has insights and resources that can reframe my concerns and questions. It is not flattering to be compared to sheep. But this comparison is true to my life. And I'll bet it is true to your life and to the communities to which you belong. If you don't believe it, just go to a congregational board meeting: Baa. Baa. Bite. Bite. Baa. "All we, like sheep, have gone astray."

I don't like to admit it, but there are times when I need a shepherd with a strong arm and a strong staff to tell me "No." I need someone to keep me from hurting myself and from hurting other people.

As I think back to my childhood, the teachers I liked most were often the ones who let me get away with the most. But the teachers who *helped* me most were the ones who knew how and when to say "No" and push me in new directions. Math classes were especially difficult. But I would not be able to balance my checkbook today if my math teachers had not continuously said "No" to many of my ways of adding and subtracting.

And in the realms of relationship, faith, and moral behavior, we sometimes need to feel the shepherd's staff. We need to come face to face with the consequences (and possible consequences) of our thoughts, feelings, and behavior. Sometimes we need to know the danger of our situation and how close we are to perishing. We must sometimes say "No" to a negative energy field, in order to participate in a positive energy field. And that choice can be difficult, no matter how promising the benefit and how necessary the change.

A little side note: The leaders of Israel are sometimes called shepherds. But there are both false and true shepherds. The false shepherds tell the people only what the people want to hear. Exploit the poor? Sure, get what you can. Practice injustice? No problem—your rights must be protected. Worship idols? Sure, you are your first priority. Israel is on the path to collapse, but the false shepherds keep saying, "Yes . . . Yes. . . Yes." They never give Israel a chance to face its problems and take the corrective action of repentance.

The true shepherds, on the other hand, make people uncomfortable in the short run. The true shepherds call the community to face its sin and repent. But beyond the discomfort is the promise of change and renewed life. The short-term "No" is part of a long-term "Yes." (For example: Ezek. 34:1-31; Jer. 23:1-4).

Other lines from the psalm come to mind. "Yea, though I walk through the valley of the shadow of death . . . thou art with me" (KJV). Or, as scholars say it should be translated: "Even were I to walk through a valley of deepest darkness . . . for you are with me" (REB). And, "Thou preparest a table before me in the presence of mine enemies" (KJV).

Well, I have made a mistake common to readers of the Bible. I was too quick to specify the meaning of a word: "I shall not want." If I had read the whole psalm more carefully, I would have realized sooner that it assumes that we will experience evil, despair, and discouragement—the valley of deepest darkness; the presence of my enemies. To recognize God as shepherd is not to pay the premium on an insurance policy that protects us against life's difficulties.

The key phrase is, "You are with me." God is with us in difficulty. God shepherds us through the tough times. When we are aware that God is with us, we have what we most need. Do you remember what the widow said? "When I say the words [of this psalm] I feel God with me."

And God is with the flood victims, and the political refugees, and the HIV/AIDS patients in their last, laboring breaths. No one dies alone.

The awareness of the divine presence can even help us respond positively and constructively to the shepherd's staff. I was told about a father, in his fifties. The last child had left home. From the outside looking it, the home appeared to have been normal and happy. But on the inside, the family members felt a lot of anger, fear, and distance. Later, the mother would say, "We were never as close as we wanted to be."

One of the adult daughters came home for a visit. In the kitchen one night, something snapped. She dropped a dish and looked at her father and accused him of sexually abusing her when she was a child. Father, daughter, mother—all in deepest darkness. The father denied it. Denial followed denial.

Pain. Suspicion. Alienation. Enemies.

The family agreed to go to a family counselor. After months of gut-wrenching therapy, he admitted that he had done the things the daughter had said. And he wept for a solid hour. That confession was the beginning of the reconstruction of their family system.

They could not remake their past. But when they brought it into the open, they gradually learned how to live with it. There were still awkward, bitter moments. But the dark secret of the past did not manipulate them as it once had.

"I couldn't have come clean," he said, "except that I knew God was with me. There were times when that was the only thing I was sure about. But it was enough."

"The LORD is my shepherd, I shall not want. . . . Even were I to walk through a valley of deepest darkness, I should fear no harm, for you are with me" (REB).

These five models are only examples of the possibilities through which teaching sermons might take shape. Homiletical theory of the last twenty-five years has increasingly emphasized the intimate relationship of form and function. The teaching function of a particular sermon might be better served by some forms than by others.

The preacher needs to determine a potentially communicative structure in the light of the subject matter, the purpose of the sermon, the patterns by which adults learn, the congregation's expectation of the sermon, and the preacher's personality. A form that may serve one occasion may not serve another. Thus, the preacher's contribution to the form of the sermon can be highly creative; the preacher not only determines what to say but how to say it in a way that has an optimum chance of receiving a hearing in the local congregation. Preachers make such determinations on the basis of their pastoral relationships with the congregation, the Christian tradition, and the culture.

The key is that the preacher must be critical of both the content of the sermon and the strengths and weaknesses of the various ways in which sermons move. In the heat of actual preaching, of course, the most ill-advised sermon can take wings, and the most carefully considered sermon can fall on the ears of the congregation like hailstones in an August thunderstorm. But, week by week, critical analysis of homiletical possibilities and limitations should result in teaching moments whose incremental impact are considerable, over the course of a long and trusted pastorate.

C H A P T E R · 6

Plans for Systematic
Teaching from the Pulpit

Teaching from the pulpit has its best effect when sermons relate systematically to one another. From week to week and month to month, sermons can build on one another. Systematic teaching allows the preacher to treat subjects in both depth and breadth. It encourages pastors to plan their sermons long in advance. This often allows homiletical ideas to simmer and season before they reach the pulpit. Spreading an important idea or complex of ideas over several Sundays allows the preacher to develop complicated notions in bite-sized pieces, so that the congregation can digest each piece before having to deal with the larger and more complex reality. The systematic preacher can take advantage of the fact that people often learn by putting together small increments of insight.

Without a systematic approach, the preacher is likely to select biblical texts, themes, doctrines, and issues in a scattershot manner. Important matters can be ignored for long periods of time. Preachers may "shoot from the hip," and focus on a limited spectrum of concerns. These concerns may be nothing more than the preacher's prejudices and biases (and sometimes these perceptions can be inconsequential). The congregation can eventually become spiritually malnourished. The listeners may begin to feel that the preacher is riding a hobbyhorse, or worse, holding them captive with a bully pulpit. Furthermore, if sermons are unrelated, the community may get the impression that God and God's purposes are unrelated. These qualities have the effect of negatively teaching the congregation.

Sometimes congregational learning takes place sequentially, as topic logically follows topic. A preacher might present a Christian doctrine and draw out its implications over the course of six weeks.

For instance, a preacher could explain the doctrine of sanctification in its biblical and historical roots, then explore its benefits for the congregation. At other times, learning takes place more on the model of a jigsaw puzzle (as discussed in the previous chapter)— piece connects with piece; developed perspectives gradually begin to emerge. For instance, over the course of several weeks, a preacher might look at a different scriptural image of the Holy Spirit each week. Regardless of whether learning is taking place in traditional linear models or in more associational patterns, learning is still enhanced when the teaching preacher plans to bring congregation and subject together in a comprehensive, systematic way.

In this chapter, I discuss six different plans for teaching systematically from the pulpit. While these are not the only possibilities, I consider them staples.

A problem: Few churchgoers are in worship every Sunday. Even the most faithful miss occasional Sundays. This situation places two requirements upon the preacher who would teach systematically from the pulpit. First, each sermon must be able to stand on its own homiletical feet. It must be a self-contained body of meaning. Each time people attend worship, they need to leave with a sense of completion. Second, the preacher can alert listeners to the place of a particular sermon in a series. This could be done by means of a brief comment at the time the Bible lesson is read, by short notes in the worship bulletin and church newsletter, or by explanatory remarks in the sermon itself.

Preaching from a Selected Lectionary

Preaching from a lectionary in the context of the Christian Year is one of the most widely used approaches in bringing a sense of order and direction to the Christian pulpit. A lectionary is thus a teaching device. The most popular lectionary in the United States today is *The Revised Common Lectionary (RCL)*.[1] The biblical readings in the *RCL* are organized in two parts:

1. From the First Sunday of Advent through Pentecost Sunday, the Christian Year is organized around seasonal cycles (Advent/Christmas/Epiphany Day; Lent/Easter/Pentecost Day).

During these periods, the Bible readings are based on *lectio selecta* (selected reading).

2. The Sundays after Epiphany, and from the Second Sunday after Pentecost to the last Sunday after Pentecost (The Reign of Christ) constitute Ordinary Time.[2] From the Second Sunday after Pentecost through The Reign of Christ, users are given a choice of readings based on *lectio continua* (continuous reading—discussed below) or on *lectio selecta*. Each has its strengths and weaknesses.

From Advent through Pentecost, the Christian Year is structured according to seasons, in order to teach specific themes of the Christian faith.[3] In Advent, the major theme is the coming of God into the world in order to redeem the world; Christmas focuses upon the incarnation of God in Christ; Epiphany Day ponders the manifestation of God through Christ; Lent shows how the life and death of Christ interpret the presence, purposes, and power of God; Easter reveals the divine purpose to initiate a new, resurrected world; Pentecost confirms that God is continually present through the Holy Spirit, to work toward the coming of the redeemed world.

The biblical readings in the *RCL* (and in most other lectionaries) are selected because they illumine these themes. The readings are drawn from a wide variety of biblical books. The *RCL* assigns four biblical readings for each Sunday. During the two great cycles, the readings assigned for each day are carefully designed so as to be related to one another.[4] The Gospel is the major reading and sets the theological theme for the day; the other readings help to interpret the themes set forth by the Gospel.[5] The fourth reading, a psalm, is appointed for liturgical use, but also can be a source of teaching from the pulpit.

Strictly speaking, the pastor does not simply teach the text. He or she preaches from the text in order to show how the text helps to broaden and deepen the community's understanding of the theme.[6] A key question for the teaching preacher: "How does this passage cast light on the particular season and on the day it is preached?"

The following are among the strengths of teaching in the pulpit from the *RCL* during the two major seasonal cycles.[7]

- During the major seasonal cycles, the *RCL* leads the congregation and preacher to texts and themes that are fundamental to the Christian faith, especially as these portray redemption through Christ. Indeed, the *RCL* encourages the church to learn and relearn the story of Jesus as the story that forms the identity of the Christian community.
- The *RCL* helps prevent the preacher from focusing on too narrow a range of texts and concerns, thereby leaving the congregation theologically deprived.
- The *RCL* brings pastor and congregation face to face with some difficult texts and issues that both pastor and people might rather avoid.
- The *RCL* keeps the Hebrew Bible alive in the consciousness of the congregation, to help it remember its Jewish heritage. The lectionary thus guards against the latent Marcionism still present in many congregations.
- The *RLC* centers on God's promises. It helps to guide the church in avoiding the trap of moralism.
- The *RCL* presumes a communal ecclesiology, which works to counteract the privatism and narcissism of late-twentieth-century North America. An expression of this communitarianism is the formation of a growing number of lectionary study groups.
- The *RCL* receives its best exposition in the context of the Lord's Supper; it is optimally designed to be a part of the full pattern of weekly word and sacrament.
- The *RCL* symbolizes the unity of the church (as many as 20 Christian communions follow it).
- The *RCL* offers the preacher practical help in sermon preparation by supplying an immediate place to begin each week. The preacher does not need to fish for a text or topic.

Yet, *The Revised Common Lectionary* has its problems. While these are not fatal, the preacher should be aware of them when considering using this approach as a basis for systematic teaching from the pulpit.

- The *RCL* subordinates the canon to the Christian Year. Scripture does not speak its own forceful word, but speaks through the theological mouthpiece of the church's calendar.

- The relationship among the biblical readings for a given Sunday is sometimes quite artificial. The preacher may sometimes be tempted to posit a relationship where none exists.
- The Hebrew Bible seldom speaks in its own voice. Unless the preacher makes a deliberate choice to preach from the First Testament, the congregation nearly always hears the First Testament in subordination to the New.
- The congregation can be confused about the relationship of the Bible readings from one week to another. When the preacher is trying to teach systematically, the congregation can become bewildered when the readings jump from Mark to John to Luke on successive Sundays.
- The Christian Year overlooks some texts and themes significant to the Christian community, especially in our era. For instance, neither the Christian year nor the *RCL* strongly emphasizes ecology.
- The prophetic emphasis on social justice is present, but does not appear as forcefully in the lectionary as it does in the Bible.
- While the lectionary leads preacher and congregation to consider some difficult texts they would rather avoid, it omits some of the most difficult, which, for that very reason, are most deserving of consideration from the pulpit.
- The beginning and ending points of some Bible readings are arbitrary; the preacher needs to be on guard for textual gerrymandering in the lectionary.

Preaching from Continuous Reading of the Bible

One of the oldest lectionary approaches to teaching from the pulpit is *lectio continua* (continuous reading). Week by week, the preacher moves seriatim through a part of the Bible, considering one passage after another in successive weeks. This pattern was probably in use in the synagogues of Palestine by the time of Jesus; very likely the rabbis read through the Torah every three years and commented on a pericope each week. This pattern was the backbone of the preaching of the teaching Reformers, particularly Luther and Calvin, and is thus eminently associated with Christian teaching.

This model is incorporated into *The Revised Common Lectionary* in Ordinary Time, especially from the Second Sunday after Pentecost through the Reign of Christ. Each synoptic Gospel provides the readings (which are sequential, but semicontinuous) for one year. Thus, the congregation follows Matthew one year, Mark the next, and Luke the next. In addition, the lectionary assigns continuous readings of the letters and other documents of the New Testament. For instance, in one year, the congregation reads much of First Corinthians in serial fashion.

The *RCL* offers two options for readings from the First Testament, and the preacher must choose between them. One set of readings correlates the First Testament readings with the Gospel reading. For instance, on the Sunday when the congregation reads the parable of the rich man and Lazarus (Luke 16:19-31), the First Testament reading is a stunning oracle of judgment on those who "lie on beds of ivory . . . and eat lambs from the flock" (Amos 6:4*a, b*).

The other set of readings from the First Testament does not correlate with the Gospel, but presents passages from the First Testament in semicontinuous readings. In one year, these trace the ancestral stories from Noah to the judges. The next year, they concentrate on the kings and wisdom literature. The third year, they focus on the prophets. (Of course, due to the length of the First Testament, the passages appointed for semicontinuous reading are merely representative.)

Thus, the *RCL* contains within itself a modified *lectio continua*. This collection of readings exposes the congregation in systematic fashion to the main bodies of literature in the Bible, and to their key passages and themes. In order to take full advantage of continuous format, of course, the preacher needs to follow the readings from one Sunday to the next, not skip from Gospel to First Testament to Epistle to psalm.

The preacher who does not follow a lectionary may find that, in the service of teaching and learning, continuous reading provides an ideal structure for bringing together congregational need and resources from the Christian tradition. Here, the key is for the preacher to discern what the congregation needs to learn and how to correlate that need with resources in the Bible. A congregation that needs to be reminded of its identity might profit from a series of sermons on Genesis which outline the identity of Israel. A community that feels as though it is in exile might profit from an extended study of Isaiah 40–55. A church that has made unholy alliances with the culture might be helped by a series of encounters with Hosea. A congregation that thinks of Jesus as little more than a moral exemplar could certainly reckon with the Johannine Jesus for a while. A community that functionally practices works righteousness would likely catch its breath after spending some time with Romans. A church that has lost hope could become realistically hopeful after living with the book of Revelation for a few weeks.

The permutations on this approach are almost endless. When preaching from a short book (such as Joel or Galatians), the pastor can preach easily not only from cover to cover, but through almost every verse. In the case of longer books (I Samuel, Ezekiel, II Corinthians, Hebrews), passages which summarize the larger themes within the book might be selected. In the case of Judges, a series of sermons that focus on the signal characters could be created. For Acts of the Apostles, the preacher might select events or speeches that unfold the story of the early Christian witness.

This approach offers distinct teaching benefits. It allows the listeners to encounter a text in depth, live in the world of the text, and let that world become a part of their consciousness. This format fits remarkably well with the recent emphasis on literary criticism in biblical scholarship; pastor and people can experience the form and function of the whole book. They can pick up its subtleties and allusions in ways that surpass those available in most one-shot sermons. Through systematic exposition, the preacher models how to study a book of the Bible. Churches on the evangelical end of the theological spectrum have found that continuous reading and preaching can be a compelling way to help the congregation encounter the gospel. I am convinced that churches in the moderate and liberal ends of the theological spectrum would be greatly strengthened by this approach.

Lectio continua also has limitations. The preacher may select parts of the Bible that restrict the congregation's theological diet. Over time, the preacher ought to take care to expose the congregation to a broad range of Scripture and theology. If a series goes on for too many Sundays, listeners can weary of it. While there are no hard and fast rules, I imagine that, in many congregations, the optimum length for focusing on one book would be about six weeks to two months.[8] Furthermore, it is easy for the preacher to concentrate on details of exegesis while losing sight of the big picture. Along the same line, the pastor can become so fascinated by exegetica that the sermon becomes boring and seemingly insignificant: "Ugh. Another lecture about the archaeology of Jericho."

Preaching on an Important Theme from the Bible or from Christian Tradition

In recent years, the most common basis for preaching has been the expounding of a single, relatively brief passage from the Bible.[9] However, some realities, ideas, images, values, or practices in the Bible and in Christian tradition and theology transcend what can be expressed in a single passage. Such ideas, images, and practices span several texts in the Bible, so that no single passage contains the fullness of the subject. I loosely refer to these interconnected motifs as themes.[10]

A theme may be developed in a single book. For instance, in the Gospel of Mark, the notion of discipleship is developed thematically. In Mark 1:16-20, the first disciples are called. The reader may naively think that the disciples are models to be emulated. But as the portraits of the disciples are drawn, readers realize that they are imperceptive and slow to respond to Jesus' teaching, hardly models to be followed. The congregation can learn from the disciples' misperceptions and failures, but they are not easy role models. Or a theme may be found within a single author or school, as in the writings of the priestly theologians, which deal with the theme of the clean and the unclean. Or a theme may occur in several different bodies of literature and stretch across Christian history, as the notion of the righteousness of God is central in Deutero-Isaiah, Matthew, Paul, and Luther. Indeed, writers in the Bible and in Christian history can have different perspectives on a similar issue.

Edward Farley points out that by preaching on isolated passages from the Bible, the preacher may do the congregation a disservice.[11] Such preaching can expose the congregation only to bits and pieces of the Bible and Christian faith, without ever helping the listeners get a sense of the Big Picture. The piece is mistaken for the whole, and the congregation may never develop a sense of the large, overarching theological realities that form the Christian faith. The congregation needs a knowledge of Christian doctrine, in the sense described in the next section, "Preaching Christian Doctrine." Without a larger theological frame of reference, the congregation is at the mercy of any text the pastor happens to be preaching.

The community may never realize that communities in the world of the Bible (and in communities of faith since) have struggled within themselves and with one another over the best understandings of vital issues.

The Deuteronomic theology, for instance, regards suffering as an indication of divine curse. The sufferer has sinned. To this, Job answers a vivid, "Not necessarily!" To preach either Deuteronomy or Job in isolation is to misrepresent the fullness of biblical conversation. Further, the preacher must reckon with the question of which perspective—if either—is more authoritative. Are there others that seem more truthful?

One way to help the congregation enlarge its awareness of such matters is to preach a series of sermons which trace a theme through the Bible and Christian history and theology, focusing on a different text or perspective each week. Along the way, the pastor should help the congregation remember that the single voice heard on a given Sunday is only one voice in the great choir of voices that take up that subject. Week by week, in the sermon itself (or in a comment at the time of Bible reading or a note in the worship bulletin), the preacher would need to remind the congregation of the place of the single sermon in the larger conversation.

As one example, a pastor might develop a series of sermons on the notion of covenant.[12] An initial sermon could focus on the meaning of *covenant* in the world of the Bible, the fact that it is given different shades of meaning in different parts of the Bible, and that it has been an important factor in the way some denominations have understood themselves. Subsequent sermons could focus on texts that are key to understanding the concept of covenant for the Christian community. The preacher might focus a sermon on each of these covenants: with Noah (Gen. 8:20-22); with Abraham and Sarah (Gen. 12:1-3, 15:1-21); at Sinai (Exod. 19:1-24:18); with David

(II Sam. 7:1-17); the new covenant (Jer. 31:31-34); the death of Jesus as having covenantal dimensions (e.g., Mark 14:22-25); the Pauline understanding of covenant (II Cor. 3:4-18); covenant in Hebrews (8:8-13, 12:18-24); the notion of covenant as constitutive of the nature of the Christian church; God's continuing covenant with the world.

Preaching a Series on Foundational Christian Doctrines

Christian maturity is centered on being able to think comprehensively, in a theological way, about what Christians believe and the implications of Christian belief for all aspects of life. The heart of Christian belief comes to a focus in Christian doctrine, the distillation of key insights from the Bible, the history of the church, contemporary experience, and reflection on core statements. Doctrine orders the bits and pieces of disparate perspectives into what is genuinely authoritative in the Christian house and what is not. Doctrine answers fundamental questions, such as: What do Christians really believe about God?; Christ?; the Holy Spirit?; the world?; the Christian life? A sermon on one such topic not only communicates the content of the doctrine, but demonstrates how to think theologically about it.

Basic doctrinal conviction helps the community discern how to locate itself in regard to questions about which the Bible or theological affirmations arrive at different points of view. For example, doctrine mediates between Job and Deuteronomy on the relationship between sin and suffering.

However, fresh circumstances and changing perspectives cause the church to be continually reassessing and, from time to time, reformulating its doctrine. The motto of the Reformed tradition is true for most Christian communities—"Reformed and always reforming." Christian doctrine is (or ought to be) always in the process of being critically examined for its adequacy and timeliness.

Christians of all churches share many doctrines in common. Yet many denominations, and even some congregations, have their own doctrinal permutations. So, whether consciously or not, pastors preach a biblical text through the lens of doctrine. In order to think critically about the relationship between the biblical text and doctrine, they need to be aware of their doctrinal position. They need to realize what that position brings to the surface in their treatment of biblical passages (and in their relationship to other matters in the Christian community), and what it tends to suppress. And the same is true for the congregation. In order to be theologically literate, the congregation needs to be able to articulate (and think critically about) its doctrine.

Pastors can focus systematically on foundational Christian doctrines. These are conveniently summarized in the great creedal formulations of the church. Thus, as Thomas G. Long says, "The once common practice of devoting a series of sermons to the principal phrases of the creed, then, looks like an old idea whose time has come again."[13] The preacher might begin with a sermon on God, then move to sermons on Christ, the Holy Spirit, the church, eternal life, the world, and how these beliefs affect the way we view issues of meaning and ethics today.

Given the theological illiteracy of many in today's church, I believe that a congregation ought to hear such a series at least once a year. The structure for the series could be taken from one of the historic formulations of the Christian faith (perhaps the Apostles' Creed) or from the denomination's more contemporary affirmation. For example, a minister in the Christian Church (Disciples of Christ) could teach from the Preamble to the Design of the Christian Church (Disciples of Christ), or from the outline of a systematic theology class from seminary days. It might be fascinating for both congregation and preacher to explore how the doctrine has changed over the centuries. What factors have prompted the community to rethink and reformulate its expression of faith?

As another possibility, the preacher could explore a single doctrine in a series of sermons, allowing both pastor and people to delve into the doctrine in detail. In a series on the Holy Spirit, the preacher might begin by outlining questions and issues that are prompted by thinking about the Holy Spirit. A sermon on the Spirit in the First Testament could highlight the Spirit's work in creation, in sustaining the world, in empowering people and communities for witness, in ecstatically filling individuals and communities. A third sermon, on the Spirit in the New Testament, could highlight the similarities and differences in the perception and work of the

Spirit in Paul, Luke, and John. A fourth sermon could trace the way the church has understood the works of the Spirit in Christian history: How have these been understood differently by different communities? What are the similarities and differences in Roman Catholic, Reformed, and Pentecostal perceptions of the Spirit? A fifth sermon might bring together the beliefs and questions of the contemporary church: What are the signs of the presence of the Spirit? How do we experience it? What does the Spirit do? How do we respond appropriately?

Preaching a Series on the Christian Interpretation of Personal and Social Issues

Christians are daily faced with important issues and phenomena that can be complicated or confusing and require Christian interpretation and response. By preaching on such issues, the pastor can both communicate solid Christian perspectives on specific phenomena and illustrate how to analyze them. Many members of the long-established denominations, however, seem not able to think clearly about such matters. They often appear to depend upon scraps of perspective from such disparate sources as isolated biblical verses (often cited without any reference to historical, literary, or theological context), media talk shows, gossip at the hair salon.

Of course, when addressing such issues, the preacher often ventures into controversial waters. Christians are not always of one mind on these matters. In such instances, it is important for the preacher to respect the different voices in the Christian community and let the congregation hear the different nuances in a fair and honest way. The community wants and needs to be informed of the strong and weak features of the different viewpoints.

· The preacher might preach a series in which each sermon focuses on a different contemporary personal or social phenomenon. The series could begin with a message that describes the resources and norms that go into a Christian evaluation of these phenomena, then focus on a different topic each week: Civil strife in other nations; whether the United States should receive refugees from other nations; homelessness in our own land; ecological concerns; Christian perspectives on postmodernism.

Or a series could focus on a single issue or phenomenon. For example, the preacher might introduce a series on the Christian nuclear (and extended) family by sketching the biblical understandings of the nature and purpose of the family, as well as its place in Christian tradition. Other sermons might focus on how family patterns and relationships today differ from those during previous centuries and the world of the Bible, or how today's family can be helped to deal with the tensions and difficulties that beset it. Another could profitably explore ways in which Christian consciousness affects our understanding of the single-parent family, as could one on the Christian family's responsibilities to its children. Such a series certainly should devote a sermon to the way single persons in the church can relate to the emphasis on family and home in the Bible and Christian tradition. And many households today would be helped with guidance into Christian possibilities for dealing with the fact of geographical separation, and with family members who are declining in health and ability for self-maintenance. A sermon could reflect on the strengths and weaknesses of thinking of the congregation as an extended family, as in the phrase "the church family."

Preaching on Questions People Ask

The preacher could put together a series of sermons that respond to questions asked by the congregation. Such an approach makes maximum use of a basic principle of adult learning articulated in chapter 3—that people are initially most interested in questions and concerns that they themselves have raised.

Preachers can become aware of these questions in two ways.[14] They can practice priestly listening throughout the course of their ministries. They are ever attentive to the issues about which people are concerned as they make pastoral calls, participate in meetings of the church, visit with people on the parking lot. They also are attentive to what is happening in the larger culture; cultural events, trends, and feelings often generate questions that can form the basis of a systematic series of sermons. Many of these would be about personal and social phenomena, as discussed in the preceding section. Others may be more subtle. For example, many people today have the impression that the United States is a culture in decline. What does it mean to live in such a culture? What is Christian hope in a situation of cultural erosion? For what does one stand?

Preachers also can become aware of the congregation's questions by asking people directly to name their concerns. A number of pastors distribute a survey instrument (in worship or through the mail) that asks the members to list the things they would like to hear addressed from the pulpit.

Some surveys limit the congregation's choices. The preacher may list several topics or texts (drawn from priestly listening) and ask the congregation to select the ones in which they are most interested. Some are open-ended. The minister simply asks, "Please name a subject, or subjects, that you would like to hear as the central focus of a sermon." This format gives the congregation the optimum opportunity to express what is consciously on its mind and heart. Pastor Richard W. Jensen entitles such a series, "You Asked for It."[15]

However, this possibility poses risks. Some of the questions may be of marginal interest to the Christian faith; others may be altogether bizarre. Occasionally, a member may be offended if the preacher does not take a certain question as the subject of a sermon. To help avoid such distractions, the pastor might explain that the large number of congregational responses makes it impossible to preach on each one. The pastor has tried to select those that appear most frequently on the surveys.

The following are sample statements from such a survey taken at a congregation in suburban Indianapolis.[16] Most of the questions appeal for help in understanding the meaning of life. The largest single body of questions, such as, "What is heaven like?" focused on eternal life. This suggests a widespread point of interest that could be addressed easily through a series of sermons on the understandings of eternal life in the Bible, in Christian history, and in theology. The second largest number of concerns had to do with the certainty of God's love and salvation: "How can I be certain that I will someday get to heaven—considering how sinful I am?" This suggests a series of sermons on the doctrine of justification by grace. Here are other illustrative questions or issues from that survey.

- I feel as if I'm part of a big rat race. Rushing around going to work. Working late. Should I be doing something different?
- What does it mean to be made in God's image?
- Why is there so much suffering among innocent people?
- What is righteousness?
- How do you get a real, working relationship with God?
- In a nonliteral interpretation of the Bible, it is confusing to me where to draw the line on what verses are applicable to our lives and what parts may be dated.
- I believe that God is omnipotent and omniscient. God knows what I am thinking and doing, and what I will be thinking and doing. If this is true, where does my free choice fit in?
- Why is there so much prejudice in God's world? Will it ever improve?
- How do we, as Christians, look at and respond to social issues, such as homosexuality—things that break the Ten Commandments?
- How do you know when God is calling you?
- How will we know when Jesus is here for the Second Coming? I fear false prophets.

Any of these questions could suggest individual sermons or could form the basis of a series. All point to the need for primary Christian teaching.

Systematic teaching from the pulpit about topics of importance signal the congregation that the preacher is thinking carefully about significant matters. The preacher's trustworthiness and credibility is enhanced. And, such teaching could have another benefit. Members of the congregation may become so interested in such a series that they resolve to hear every sermon!

C H A P T E R • 7

Teaching a Core Curriculum from the Pulpit

Staple stories, ideas, and realities of the Christian faith need to be taught and learned in every generation. All Christians need to know the basic narratives of the Bible and the key doctrines of Christianity, in order to be able to function minimally as Christians. From time to time, however, some motifs need particularly to be emphasized. For instance, at the time of Luther, the church needed to rediscover justification by grace through faith. Without that conviction at its heart, the church is in theological trouble.

In this chapter, I posit some emphases that seem to me to be urgent for our time. These emphases need to be taught from the pulpits of many congregations in the long-established churches, since they arise from the climate of theological depletion found in many such communities. The list cannot be exhaustive, but I touch on material that is basic to helping a congregation develop the maturity of theological consciousness that will help it recognize and respond to the living God as known through Jesus Christ, and make sense of issues of meaning and ethics.

I have tried to frame issues that need to be addressed, regardless of the theological orientation of the preacher and the congregation. For example, each preacher and congregation should come to a clear conclusion regarding their view of authority in the church, in light of their deepest convictions about God and the world. However, my own theological biases inevitably creep into the presentation. Therefore, it is important to acknowledge that pastors whose theological perspectives differ from mine will perceive the specific content of these issues in accordance with their own theologies. A strict biblicist, for instance, will resolve the issue of authority along a different axis. Nonetheless, regardless of theological orientation, these are basic issues with which preachers and congregations need to wrestle.

Some of this material has come to expression in earlier contexts. I call attention to it now in order to highlight its importance. These are subjects that need explicit attention from the Christian pulpit. I have tried to avoid making a shopping list of the latest social fads and events, and concentrate on basic matters that are likely to be a part of the church's agenda into the twenty-first century.

Authority

Authority may be the single most important issue in the contemporary church. Authority is that "reality on which confidence and responsible decisions turn. An authority is a point of reference, a locus of credibility which gives direction and abiding character to human life."[1] On what authorities does the church rely as it makes its judgments about matters of Christian interpretation? What is the nature of the preacher's authority? And what is the authority of the church as it witnesses in the contemporary setting? The issue of authority is manifest in two levels in the church today.

At one level, authority is one of the central dividing points among Christian people and communities.[2] At this level, the issue is intimately related to sources of the knowledge of God, discussed in the next section of this chapter. Churches toward the theological right maximize the authority of the Bible (and their interpretation of the Bible), and minimize the authority of tradition and experience.[3] The community's business is to understand the Bible and order its life under it.[4] Moving toward the theological left, churches honor the Bible but increasingly regard tradition, experience, and reason as authoritative. On the left, authoritative interpretation of Christian faith and behavior is determined through conversation within the community. Many members of the long-established churches are confused about the differences between their congregations and those of the newer churches, whose witnesses appear to be rather different. The preacher can help the congregation understand these differences by preaching on how the different churches understand the notion of authority.

However, the issue of authority has a deeper level. Why should the contemporary postmodern community take seriously the claims of Christian faith? Only a generation ago, most in the congregation would recognize external authorities (for example, the Bible, the call of the preacher, ordination) as sufficient reason for heeding the preacher and the Christian message. However, as Edward Farley trenchantly points out, this house of authority has collapsed.[5]

Two of the hallmarks of postmodern culture are pluralism and relativism.[6] Many viewpoints exist side by side in the marketplace of interpretation of the meaning of life. Why should contemporary people invest in a pattern of meaning centered in a Jewish male who was crucified almost two millenia ago? In our society, feelings have become a basic norm by which we make decisions. "Why did you do that?" "Because it felt good." "Why won't you do this?" "Because it doesn't feel good." Why should people be attracted to a religion that includes the possibility of feelings of rejection and calls for hard, clear thinking about life's most difficult (and often painful) realities?

Therefore, the preacher needs to develop patterns of internal authority. Why should the community take seriously the claims of the Bible and Christian faith? Ministers need to make a case for what they are asking the congregation to believe. Why should a congregation regard a message as true?

In this respect, today's clergy may be called to relearn how to engage in apologetics, the act of making a defense for the faith. As First Peter says, it is making a "defense . . . for the hope that is in you" (3:15). Apologetics can show why the Christian faith is reasonable. In our time, apologetic preaching would not be focused on those outside the church, to persuade them of the truth of Christianity, but initially would be focused on the church itself. In the manner of Anselm's faith seeking understanding, the preacher would try to help the congregation understand why Christian professions are believable. For instance, can the preacher help the congregation understand why it should continue to believe in an eschatological hope, in the face of two thousand years of unrelenting misery, suffering, and death?

A congregation would be well served, both by hearing entire sermons which explore generally the notion of authority, and by hearing sermons in which the preacher shows why specific texts and theological prescriptions can be regarded as authoritative. Indeed, in the process of preparing sermons, a preacher could regularly ask, "Why should the congregation take seriously this text (or doctrine or theological point of view)?"

Sources of Our Knowledge of God

The knowledge of God, and of God's purposes, is fundamental to Christian identity. Few in the long-established churches are sufficiently familiar with the sources of our knowledge of God and with how to draw on them. If the church is to talk about God (and about what God offers the world and requires of it), then Christians need to know what we can say about God, and what we cannot. By preaching on the sources of our knowledge of God, the preacher helps the congregation develop a dual sense of confidence in its capacity to understand God, and recognition of limitation in its capacity to do so. The preacher can encourage the congregation to understand the content and character of the sources and how to employ them. As indicated earlier, these sources are the Bible, Christian tradition, and experience, all brought together by reason.

Historically, the church has regarded the *Bible* as the most important source of the knowledge of God. As noted earlier, the preacher needs to help the congregation become aware of the content of the Bible. A problem: The Bible is not a single book but a library; it is not a single source, but a collection of sources, each interpreting the presence and purposes of God at different moments or from different perspectives. Some voices in the Bible offer different viewpoints on the same or on similar issues. The preacher must help the congregation learn how to recognize these different viewpoints and mediate between them.

Furthermore, the preacher needs to help the congregation learn how to span the gap in worldview between the worlds of the Bible and our worlds.

Beyond this hermeneutical problem, however, a growing number of Christians today believe that the Bible contains some material that does not witness to the living God, but reflects the finite and flawed perspectives of communities of antiquity. The preacher needs to help the congregation evaluate the witness of biblical texts.

The term *Christian tradition* (in this context) refers to Christian interpretation, outside of the Bible, to the present day. This consists of the voices, events, and experiences of Christians through the ages.[7] Tradition can be regarded as a source of the knowledge of God, because God is omnipresent. People can become aware of God's presence and purposes in any moment. Through the centuries, the church has discovered that some Christians have become unusually aware of aspects of the divine presence and have been able to articulate their awareness so as to enlarge the church's understanding of God.

A problem: The tradition is not a single source, but a portfolio of the different ways Christians have interpreted God's presence. As in the case of the Bible, the preacher has a double job description. First, it is to help the congregation become familiar with the content of the tradition. This may seem an overwhelming task. After all, the tradition has been building for two thousand years and is increasing exponentially year by year, thanks to the wonders of contemporary publishing. It may encourage the preacher's sense of adequacy to envision the task in small pieces. Much of the learning needs to take place in classes and other settings outside the sanctuary. The tradition is too big to be covered in twenty-minute segments once a week. Further, week by week, the preacher can indicate the way key voices in the tradition have interpreted the biblical text or doctrine on which the sermon is based.[8] From time to time, the preacher also could preach an entire sermon (or series of sermons) on key figures in the tradition. For example, a United Methodist might preach on key insights into the Christian faith from Susanna, John, and Charles Wesley.

Relative to the tradition, the second part of the preacher's job description is to help the congregation sort through those aspects of the tradition that seem more and less authoritative, and determine why they seem so.

Experience, as we commented in chapter 4, is what really happens to us in the world. As in the previous instance of the tradition, the underlying theological conviction is that God is omnipresent. Therefore, we can become aware of divine participation in the world through our own experience in the world. The church habitually has focused on experience at two levels.

At the macro level, what we observe in the world can alert us to God. Many Christians, for instance, believe that nature reveals clues to the divine will. Social movements, such as the long struggle for liberation in South Africa, also can point to the divine will.

At the micro level, the inner life—our feelings, our intuitions, our thoughts—can mediate the knowledge of God. When receiving the bread and the cup, for instance, I frequently feel a fullness in my heart that I take to be a response to the overflowing fullness of God.

A problem: How can Christians distinguish those aspects of experience that disclose the divine, and those that obfuscate or actually work against it?

The preacher again has a dual calling. One phase is to help the congregation learn to name its experience in the larger world, and also within its own mind and heart. The social sciences (especially psychology, sociology, economics, political analysis) and the arts often are particularly illuminating at this juncture. The other phase of the preacher's job is to help the community evaluate its experiences, to determine whether they seem to make known the divine presence and purposes or seem to frustrate those purposes.

The pastor can make experience the focal point of preaching. What is experience? The preacher could point out that experience has given rise to texts and doctrines, and also has called some of those very formulations into question. The preacher could help the congregation become more sensitive to both macro experience and micro experience. (Many people, after all, do not perceive clearly what really is happening to them, nor are they reflective about its significance). The sermon might point to people past and present who have been attuned to their own experience, and to the possibilities and pitfalls of turning to experience as a source of knowledge of God.

The church sometimes speaks of *reason* as another source of the knowledge of God. Strictly speaking, reason is not a singular source, but is the function of making sense of the three main sources. Reason operates in every theological system. It helps pastor and people determine those aspects of Christian conviction that are credible, and those that are incredible. It guides the community to consider items of Christian belief that relate logically to one another, and those that may be contradictory. Reason helps the community determine what fits inside the community's current worldview, and what does not. It also rings a bell that warns the community that its worldview needs to shift, in response to fresh perceptions.

A key, of course, is for the preacher to help the congregation understand that all our conclusions regarding the knowledge of God are instances of *interpretation*.[9] We do not encounter pure reality in an uninterpreted state. Human consciousness always interprets the data that come to it from the world outside the self, and also from the world inside the self. As Alfred North Whitehead said, "If we desire a record of uninterpreted experience, we must ask a stone to record its autobiography."[10] The preacher can help the congregation understand that all statements about God and God's purposes for the world are interpretive. This is why the Christian community is perpetually examining its convictions: We seek to respond to new insights and data that may lead the church to enlarge or revise its interpretive tradition. This again points the pastor in binary directions: Regularly, the preacher ought to help the congregation understand the strenghts of its present interpretation of reality, but also ought to help it recognize the relativities inherent in its interpretation of the divine presence and aims.

The Core of the Christian Vision

It is important for the preacher, in every generation, to teach and reteach the core of the Christian vision, the gospel. As noted earlier, my colleague Clark Williamson formulates the gospel in a way that is recognizable in virtually every Christian community. The gospel is "the good news that God graciously and freely offers the divine love to each and all (oneself included) and that this God who loves all the creatures therefore *commands* that justice be done to them." The gospel is thus dipolar: It "(a) *promises* God's love to each of us as the only adequate ground of our life and (b) *demands* justice from us toward *all* others whom God loves."[11]

Why is it important for the pastor to teach the core of the Christian vision again and again? The answer is very simple:

because the community tends not only to forget its center, but to corrupt it.

The church in our time falls prey to three particular corrosions. The first is works righteousness.[12] In the mode of works righteousness, the church shifts the focus of the gospel from God's initiatives to our response. We must do certain things (works) in order to be accepted in the circle of God's love. Certain sectors of the church emphasize works that are primarily individual in character; if I observe traditional sexual mores, work hard, and am a good citizen, I can be one of God's friends. Other sectors of the church emphasize works that are more social in expression; I must identify with the proper social movements if I am to be included in God's love. In some Christian circles, participation in social witness is the contemporary indulgence. Such emphases, of course, sever the main artery that feeds Christian life. Few Christians (including preachers) consciously make a commitment to works righteousness, and this lack of recognition makes it all the more insidious.

Another corrosion is closely related: moralism. Moralism emphasizes the *demand* of the gospel, to the detriment of the *promise* of the gospel. Indeed, a moralistic pastor can reduce the gospel to prescriptions for moral behavior.[13] The up side of this emphasis, of course, is that it encourages Christians to put faith into practice. The down side is that Christian life can become little more than a matter of moral action. The moralist can lose the sense of Transcendent Reality, with its intimate relationship to humankind and nature.

Still another corrosion is cheap grace. A preacher may emphasize God's unconditional love without calling sufficient attention to the fact that acceptance of God's love bestows an identity which requires the practice of love in all relationships. The preacher who advocates cheap grace assures the congregation of God's good pleasure toward it, but does not help it recognize how to respond to this love. A preacher actually can use cheap grace to comfort people who participate in patterns of cruelty; the pastor assures them of God's love without calling them to be loving toward all others.

Beyond these specific corrosions, the congregation can be filled with all manner of versions of the gospel and maxims for proper and improper Christian behavior, versions and maxims that originate without reference to the Bible, Christian tradition, or theology. False gospels circulate in popular piety—through the media, over the fence, in the coffee klatch—and often they have more authority in the consciousness of the congregation than the full-bodied gospel.

The preacher needs to remind the congregation frequently of the content of the gospel and help it work out the gospel's implications. The pastor also needs to help the congregation recognize the limited versions of ultimate reality that often play on its channels of consciousness. And preachers need to check their preaching regularly for emphases that underrepresent or misrepresent the gospel.

How to Think Theologically

Theologians today use the notion of thinking theologically to refer to being able to analyze a biblical text, doctrine, idea, or situation, in the light of clear Christian convictions and norms. Indeed, theological thinking is an instance of critical thinking (as discussed in chapter 3). The theological thinker is able to identify alternative modes of interpretation, describe their strengths and weaknesses, and choose those that are more or less commendable. The critical thinker can especially make sense of pieces of data that conflict with one another. A critically thinking congregation can describe a belief or phenomenon in both its surface and depth dimensions.

A congregation that can think theologically has a mature understanding of authority, of the sources of our knowledge of God, and of the core of the Christian vision. All of these contribute to a theological method which the congregation can employ to think through its perception of ideas and situations. Without a systematic method of evaluation, a community may be frustrated as to where to begin, how to proceed, and how to draw conclusions. A community might well have several key insights into a biblical . passage, a theological notion or a personal or social situation, but be unsure about what judgments are at home (or not at home) in the Christian house.

One reason the contemporary church has such difficulty dealing with whether homosexuality can be a Christian orientation is that the church does not have a well-defined program for thinking theologically. The church is caught in a sometimes confusing and contradictory web of data. The Bible, for instance, has little to say about homosexuality. Most (if not all) of the Bible's teaching is negative. However, homosexual relationships in the Bible are not parallel to the best of homosexual relationships today. The tradition is largely negative on the subject of homosexuality, except for a few exceptional voices. Data from today's social and biological sciences can be lined up on both sides of the question. Some suggests that homosexuality is an innate state of being. Other data suggests that it is a learned behavior.

The experience of some contemporary homosexuals has been quite negative. They ask how it could be otherwise, when they are forced into a despised subculture and must practice their sexuality in secret. However, an increasing number of homosexuals testify that their relationships are positive and fulfilling (and become more so as they become more socially acceptable). Indeed, they argue that their relationships are covenantal, in the biblical sense. Further, homosexuality is emotionally sensitive.

Unfortunately, some contemporary Christians come to conclusions about the possibility of homosexuality as a Christian lifestyle on the basis of partial awareness of the data. Indeed, some base their theological judgments on nothing more than a handful of Bible verses or the latest report from a scientific journal. Small wonder that homosexuality is one of the most divisive issues in the church, here in the closing years of the twentieth century. The church needs a way to make a critical way through this maze.

I commend a particular approach, a simplified adaptation of the path to preparing a teaching sermon outlined in chapter 3:

1. The congregation describes the biblical text, the Christian belief, or the personal or social phenomenon that is the focus of theological analysis. In order to make an evaluation of an idea or state of affairs, the congregation needs to have a clear picture of what it is evaluating. What are the surface elements of the text, doctrine, or situation? What are the deeper elements? In order to respond sufficiently to these questions, the congregation may need to consult outside resources—Bible commentaries or data from

psychology or sociology. In this process, the interpreting body needs to be aware that its own prejudices and biases may contribute (both negatively and positively) to its description and analysis.

2. The congregation asks: Is this reality (biblical text, Christian conviction, personal or corporate circumstance) appropriate to the gospel? The congregation needs to know whether the phenomenon is consistent with the core of the Christian vision. Does the subject manifest God's love for all, and call for justice for all?

3. The congregation asks: Is this reality intelligible? Is it consistent with other things that Christians say and do which are appropriate to the gospel? Does it make sense in the light of the contemporary worldview? Does it challenge an aspect of the contemporary worldview?[14] In responding to these questions, the congregation may need to draw on sources of the knowledge of God. For example, the church's contemporary experience of the subject (or the church's evaluation of the experience of others) may cause the church to question some aspect of its worldview.

4. The congregation asks: Is this reality morally plausible? Does it call for the moral treatment of all concerned? Specifically, does it call for all involved to be treated with love?

5. The congregation summarizes its theological analysis of the subject. What position should the congregation take in regard to the subject?

The preacher can do two things to help the community develop a self-conscious theological method. The first is to preach about the importance of thinking theologically and about how to do so. The other is to model theological thinking in the course of sermons which focus on the interpretation of a biblical text, doctrine, or situation.

I hasten to add that a clear theological method will not resolve every facet of every problem. Our finite perceptions cannot always penetrate to the depths necessary for understanding complex matters. Those who introduce theological method into the congregation should not pretend to control its outcome; the members of the congregation need to learn to think together as a community. However, at the very least, a good theological analysis can help the congregation identify the key points at issue and the possibilities for interpretation. The community then has a critical frame of reference for making decisions about its beliefs and actions.

The Nature and Purpose of the Church

In the United States, the relationship between church and culture has changed over the past fifty years. At midcentury, church and culture lived in an informal, but very powerful alliance, in which their values and practices were perceived to be mutually supportive. The church blessed the nation (its democratic form of government, its capitalistic economic system, its values of freedom). Some even spoke of the United States as a Christian nation. Historians sometimes used the term *Christendom* to describe this state of affairs. The purposes of the church were to help people become good citizens and help to build a better world. Church membership (and the ministry as a vocation) was socially valued. The success of the church could be measured along the same lines as that of other community institutions. The church had the ear of public officials. Many people perceived the nation as a homogenous social fabric. A fair number of Christians (particularly those in the older strata of the church's membership) still think along these lines.

However, the situation is dramatically different today.[15] In the United States, the church no longer has favored cultural status. Pluralism is a buzzword for our time. In a pluralistic society, different religions exist side by side; none is more favored than another; each must make its own claims for truth and human loyalty. Indeed, the culture no longer assumes that religion ought to be a part of its mainstream.

This situation means that congregations need to give renewed attention to their purpose. Most would agree with Joe R. Jones' general statement of the nature and purpose of the church: "The church is that community of persons called into being by the gospel of Jesus Christ to witness in word and deed to the living God for the benefit of the world."[16] The purpose of the church is to witness to the presence, purpose, and power of God. The church needs to help the congregations differentiate between the relativities, falsehoods, and idolatries of the world, and the certainties, truth, and transcendence that emanate from God. The church, in turn, witnesses to these realities in its larger cultural setting.

The long-established churches are currently divided on how best to make this witness.[17] Some, represented by Stanley Hauerwas and William Willimon, believe that the church should remain basically a colony that carries out its interior life of worship, study, and pastoral upbuilding, and that engages in ministries beyond the congregation that demonstrate God's love for the world.[18] In this view, the church seldom goes into the public arena to make its witness as one entity of society alongside others. The church lets its light shine through the quality of its life. Those outside the church should be able to see the light and be attracted to its vision for the world.[19]

Others, represented by David Tracy, believe that the church should order its interior life so that it can be shaped by the gospel. In addition, the church takes its witness into the public arena.[20] The church joins other institutions in the community to discuss the (relatively) best ways to order community life. The church seeks a world in which all relationships and possibilities are shaped by love and justice.[21] The church offers its contributions as a conversation partner, not as an imperial voice from on high. In the public marketplace, the church risks its understanding of God's purposes for the world; it must make a case for its recommendations on the basis of evidence and arguments that persons outside the church will find acceptable. The encounter of the gospel with the public arena sometimes causes the church to reconsider its conviction. Of course, the church must sometimes call a spade a spade. It must sometimes simply say that the culture is fomenting falsehood, injustice, idolatry, and death. In this view, the church exists for the public good.

The preacher can help the community grasp these different ways of assessing the purpose of the church and their resulting implications for shaping the day-to-day ministry of the congregation. Which seems more compelling? What are some practical strategies for implementing either vision in the church program—and in witness outside the congregation?

A caution: When preaching on the nature and purpose of the church, clergy sometimes give the impression that the church is primarily concerned with its own institutional maintenance. The building up of the church is sometimes represented as an end in itself. Both positions above essentially regard the church as a community of witness. The preacher needs to help the congregation develop a consciousness of its life as being a pointer toward the living God, whose purposes are for the whole of the cosmos.

Basic Christian Doctrines

Congregations in theological anemia (or in theological amnesia) need transfusions of basic Christian doctrine. What can the church believe about God? Jesus Christ? The Holy Spirit? The Trinity? What is sin? Grace? Judgment? Law? Sanctification? What is the purpose of the church? The purpose of the Christian life? What is the significance of baptism? The breaking of bread? What theological ideas are distinctive of the congregation's denomination (or other affiliation)?

In the previous chapter, we considered plans for systematically helping the congregation learn the content of Christian doctrine and its application for life. I mention this subject again to underscore its importance.

Interpretation of Current Personal and Social Phenomena

The congregation needs to know how to make Christian sense of the world in which it is living, and of the daily lives of its members. What does God offer? What does God ask? The preacher is thus called to lead the congregation in the interpretation of current personal and social phenomena, from the perspective of the gospel.

By personal phenomena, I mean matters that we perceive as taking place largely within our personal sphere. These include an individual's feelings, interpersonal relationships, family affairs, and personal hopes, gains, and losses. By social phenomena, I refer to issues and realities that are manifest in the larger culture of which we are a part. These are illustrated by racism, by the media culture, by concern for health care.

Of course, it is artificial to speak of personal and social issues as if they are in different arenas. Life is an interconnected web; social realities shape the environment within which personal life takes place. My own feelings, attitudes, possibilities, and limitations are deeply affected by culture-wide realities. My attitudes and behaviors contribute to the formation of larger cultural realities. If I join a march to protest United States' reluctance to offer safe haven to certain groups of refugees, I help to shape a social attitude and policy. As David Buttrick points out, the categories of personal and social are largely matters of emphasis.[22]

One would suppose that these matters come up frequently in Christian preaching. Preachers do mention them, but seldom do they make them the focus of whole sermons. According to a recent study of more than 200 sermons preached in the Christian Church (Disciples of Christ), only 5 percent of the sermons focus in a thorough and systematic way on an issue of social justice. Only 3 percent focus in a thorough and systematic way on other social issues.[23] The pastor may frequently mention issues of justice and other social issues, but such references usually occur as subsidiary points; they are seldom the central subject matter of the sermon. For instance, preachers tend to use homosexuality as an illustration, rather than as the primary locus of the sermon's content. This suggests that the time may be right for helping the congregations learn how to think about (and live through) major current issues. It further suggests that aspects of the prophetic witness of the church are being underplayed.

Preachers do not want the Sunday sermon to be a rehash of the previous week's lead stories from the evening news. But they should regularly assay the basic issues that face the congregations in their kitchens, playgrounds, and workplaces. Are their sermons helping the people learn Christian perspectives on these topics? Similarly, pastors should take note of culture-wide factors. Are their sermons helping the congregations understand and respond to these phenomena? In the previous chapter, we outlined possible plans to systematically teach these topics from the pulpit.

I could become ever more specific. The church is called to respond to things ranging from ecology to the emerging multicultural social world, to various forms of human abuse and oppression, to the emerging roles of women and men, to the interconnectedness of all persons and communities, to consideration of stunning new scientific discoveries, to modes of spirituality that are suited to the late 1990s. But all these and more should come to the preacher's attention as part of pastoral listening. And all have this in common: The church thinks about all of them (and everything else too), from the standpoint of God's presence and purposes.

In order to be reliable guides, teaching preachers must continuously cultivate a vital relationship with God. This prepares them with content for Christian teaching, and also with a source of strength for those occasions when Christian teaching brings preacher and congregation into tension. And it provides each preacher with the knowledge of a Great Companion who is present in all phases of preparation and teaching. Indeed, the Teacher of All Teachers rejoices more than anyone else when Christian teaching takes root and grows.

APPENDIX

Sample Worksheet
for Developing the Sermon
As an Event of Teaching and Learning

1. Identify a point at which the congregation needs to learn.[1]
   What do we, as a congregation, most need to learn this week, as part of our growth in Christian understanding and action?
2. Determine the basic issues and questions that are essential to understand and preach on the subject.
3. Investigate resources needed to understand the subject:
   a. The Bible
   b. Christian history from the Bible to the present
   c. Contemporary studies in theology, psychology, sociology, economics, politics, and so on.
   d. Arts
4. Come to a Christian understanding of the subject.
   a. What is an understanding that is appropriate to the gospel?
   b. What is an understanding that is intelligible?
   c. What is an understanding that is morally plausible?
5. Describe the congregation's relationship to the subject.
   a. Is the congregation informed and enthusiastic?
   b. Is the congregation favorably inclined toward the subject, but with an inadequate understanding or experience or knowledge of how to act?
   c. Is the congregation informed or experienced, but acting out of character?
   d. Is the congregation apathetic?
   e. Is the congregation unfavorably inclined, even resistant to new possibilities of understanding, experience, or action?
6. Determine what you hope will happen in the hearts, minds, and wills of the listeners, as a result of hearing the sermon.

a. What do you hope the congregation will understand? How do you hope it will enlarge, reinforce, or correct the congregation's Christian perception or living?

b. What do you hope the congregation will experience or feel?

c. How do you hope the congregation will act in response to the sermon?

7. Summarize the content of the sermon in a single indicative sentence.

Subject: God

Verb: Activity of God for the benefit of the world

Predicate: Result of God's activity (and, perhaps, our response to the awareness of that activity).

8. List the memories, questions, and other matters that are likely to be on the hearts and minds of the listeners as they interact with the sermon.

a. Memories?

b. Questions?

c. Beliefs?

d. Experiences?

e. Predispositions, prejudices?

f. Preachers should answer these questions for themselves.

9. Plan the content and movement of the sermon so that the congregation will have a good opportunity to learn what it needs to learn.

a. When the congregation is informed and enthusiastic, the preacher can build on the knowledge and enthusiasm for larger, deeper, understanding and practice.

b. When the congregation is favorably inclined but has inadequate understanding or experience or response in action, the preacher must search for ways to supplement or correct the congregation's present state.

c. When the congregation is informed but acting out of character, the preacher needs to help it perceive the contradiction and want to make a correction.

d. When the congregation is apathetic, the preacher can use homiletical approaches to help it discover the importance and significance of the subject.

e. When the congregation is unfavorably inclined toward the subject, or even resistant to it, the preacher can help it overcome this resistance and see positive benefits in new ways of understanding or acting.

10. Draw on styles and qualities of learning that can enhance the congregation's participation in the sermon.[2]

NOTES

Introduction

1. A version of this incident appeared in Ronald J. Allen, "The Teaching Church," *Preaching* vol. 9, no. 1 (1993), p. 49.
2. Clark M. Williamson and Ronald J. Allen, *The Teaching Minister* (Louisville: Westminster/John Knox Press, 1991).
3. John C. Holbert and Ronald J. Allen, *Holy Root, Holy Branches: Christian Preaching from the First Testament* (Nashville: Abingdon Press, 1995).

1. The Call to the Teaching Ministry Today

1. Andrae Lemaire, "Education (Israel)," *The Anchor Bible Dictionary*, ed. David N. Freedman et al. (New York: Doubleday, 1992), vol. 2, pp. 305-12.
2. On how the Old Testament teaches, see Walter Brueggemann, *the Creative Word* (Philadelphia: Fortress Press, 1982).
3. For a current concise overview, see Eugene Wehrli, *Gifted by The Spirit* (Cleveland: Pilgrim Press, 1992), pp. 61-80.
4. Werner Jaeger, *Paideia*, trans. Gilbert Highet (New York: Oxford University Press, 1939–1945), 3 vols. On education in the ancient world, see H. I. Marrou, *A History of Education in Antiquity*, trans. George Lamb (New York: Sheed & Ward, 1956).
5. Werner Jaeger, *Early Christianity and Paideia* (Cambridge: Harvard University Press, 1961).
6. David H. Kelsey, *To Understand God Truly* (Louisville: Westminster/John Knox Press, 1992), p. 69.
7. Ibid., pp. 67, 73.
8. Richard R. Osmer, *A Teachable Spirit* (Louisville: Westminster/John Knox Press, 1990), pp. 73-83.
9. Ibid., pp. 84-135.
10. Martin Luther, *Table Talk,* cited by Wilhelm Pauck, "Ministry in the Time of the Continental Reformation," *The Ministry in Historical Perspective,* ed. H. Richard Niebuhr and Daniel D. Williams (New York: Harper & Brothers, 1956), p. 134.

11. Fred W. Meuser, *Luther the Preacher* (Minneapolis: Augsburg Publishing House, 1983), p. 17.
12. John Calvin, *Institutes of the Christian Religion*, Vol. 2, ed. John T. NcNeill, trans. Ford L. Battles (Philadelphia: The Westminster Press, 1960), pp. 1016-21, 1053-58.
13. T. H. L. Parker, *Calvin's Preaching* (Louisville: Westminster/John Knox Press, 1992), pp. 35, 107.
14. For instance, these themes weave in and out of Horton Davies, *Worship and Theology in England* (Princeton: University Press, 1961–70), as in vol. 2, pp. 133-84, and his *The Worship of the American Puritans 1629–1730* (New York: Peter Lang, 1990), pp. 77-114. For other examples, see Merrill R. Abbey, *The Epic of United Methodist Preaching* (Lanham, Md.: University Press of America, 1984), p. 2; Thomas A. Langford, "The Teaching Office in The United Methodist Church," *Quarterly Review*, vol. 10, no. 3 (1990), pp. 4-17; and Granville T. Walker, *Preaching in the Thought of Alexander Campbell* (St. Louis: Bethany Press, 1954), pp. 156-66.
15. For the data of decline, see Wade Clark Roof and William McKinney, *American Mainline Religion* (New Brunswick: Rutgers University Press, 1987).
16. Ibid., pp. 164-70.
17. See ibid., pp. 11-39, and Robert Wuthnow, *The Restructuring of American Religion* (Princeton: University Press, 1988). For a brief popular exposition, see Loren Meade, *The Once and Future Church* (Washington, D.C.: The Alban Institute, 1991).
18. Roof and McKinney, *American Mainline Religion*, p. 170.
19. Ibid., pp. 16, 176, 180-81.
20. D. Newell Williams, "Future Prospects of the Christian Church (Disciples of Christ)," *A Case Study of Mainstream Protestantism*, ed. D. Newell Williams (Grand Rapids: William B. Eerdmans/St. Louis: Chalice Press, 1991), p. 562. See similarly, Milton J. Coalter, John M. Mulder, and Louis B. Weeks, *The Presbyterian Presence* (Louisville: Westminster/John Knox Press, 1990–92), 7 vols.
21. Peter L. Benson and Carolyn H. Elkin, *Effective Christian Education: A National Study of Protestant Congregations* (Minneapolis: Search Institute, 1990), p. 3. For difficulties in the Institute's definition of faith and its research methodology, see *Rethinking Christian Education*, ed. David S. Schuller (St. Louis: Chalice Press, 1993).
22. See Jaroslav Pelikan, *The Vindication of Tradition* (New Haven: Yale University Press, 1984), pp. 3-21.
23. Joseph E. Faulkener, "What Are They Saying? A Content Analysis of 206 Sermons Preached in the Christian Church (Disciples of Christ) During 1988," *A Case Study of Mainstream Protestantism*, ed. Williams, p. 416. The sermons were chosen according to social sciences' standard practices in identifying scientifically reliable research samples.

24. John McClure, "Changes in the Authority, Method and Message in Presbyterian (UPCUSA) Preaching in the Twentieth Century," *The Confessional Mosaic: Presbyterians and Twentieth-Century Theology*, ed. Milton J. Coalter, John M. Mulder, and Louis B. Weeks (Louisville: Westminster/John Knox Press, 1990), pp. 108, 280 (n. 96).
25. For an instrument to help gauge the consistency of theological expression in one's preaching, see J. Randall Nichols, *Building the Word* (San Francisco: Harper & Row, 1980), p. 135.
26. For an overview of the literature, see Allison Stokes and David A. Roozen, "The Unfolding Story of Congregational Studies," *Carriers of Faith*, ed. Carl S. Dudley, Jackson W. Carroll, and James P. Wind (Louisville: Westminster/John Knox Press, 1991), pp. 183-92.
27. On this point, see Clark M. Williamson and Ronald J. Allen, *The Teaching Minister* (Louisville: Westminster/John Knox Press, 1991), pp. 105-24.
28. These are discussed in detail in Eugene C. Roehlkepartain, *The Teaching Church* (Nashville: Abingdon Press, 1993), pp. 57-71.
29. Charles Wesley, "Love Divine, All Loves Excelling," *The United Methodist Hymnal* (Nashville: The United Methodist Publishing House, 1989), p. 384.
30. Wade Clark Roof, *A Generation of Seekers* (San Francisco: HarperCollins, 1993), pp. 147-48.
31. Ibid., p. 156, 192, 204-12, 185.
32. For instance, Robert Kegan, *The Evolving Self* (Cambridge: Harvard University Press, 1982), pp. 1-12; Leon McKenzie, *Adult Education and Worldview Construction* (Malabar, Fla.: Krieger Publishing Co., 1991), pp. 1-16. Laurent Daloz, *Effective Teaching and Mentoring* (San Francisco: Jossey-Bass, 1986), pp. 1-15, shows that the search for meaning is a primary motive for adult learning.
33. Lyle Schaller, *21 Bridges to the 21st Century* (Nashville: Abingdon Press, 1994), p. 84.
34. Lyle Schaller, *44 Steps Up Off the Plateau* (Nashville: Abingdon Press, 1993), p. 86.
35. James Fish, "Teaching as We Preach: Education for the Sake of Mission," *Currents in Theology and Mission* 18 (1991), p. 357.
36. Robert Wuthnow explores the relationship between theology and style of religious discourse in *Rediscovering the Sacred* (Grand Rapids: William B. Eerdmans, 1992), pp. 59-82.
37. Clifford Geertz, *The Interpretation of Cultures* (New York: Basic Books, 1973), pp. 87-125.
38. Lyle Schaller, "How Long Is the Sermon?" *The Parish Paper*, vol. 1, no. 11 (1994), pp. 1-2.
39. Richard F. Ward offers an excellent analysis of factors that enhance communication in *Speaking from the Heart: Preaching with Passion* (Nashville: Abingdon Press, 1992).

40. See William H. Willimon, "Preaching: Entertainment or Exposition," *The Christian Century* 107 (1990), pp. 204-6.

2. What Is a Teaching Sermon?

1. On naming, see Peter L. Berger and Thomas Luckmann, *The Social Construction of Reality* (Garden City: Doubleday, 1966), pp. 85-96. In the language of Berger and Luckmann, the Christian teacher posits a Christian symbolic universe with the congregation.
2. The best discussion of experience known to me is Bernard Meland, esp. *Fallible Forms and Symbols* (Philadelphia: Fortress Press, 1976), pp. xiii-xiv, 54-57, 185-89, and his earlier works.
3. Richard R. Osmer, "Review of *The Teaching Minister*," *The Princeton Seminary Bulletin* 13 (1992), p. 247. Osmer contrasts the teaching church with the pastoral church, "which focuses primarily on meeting people's needs."
4. Northrop Frye, *The Great Code* (New York: Harcourt, Brace, Jovanovich, 1982), p. xv.
5. Mary C. Boys, "Teaching: The Heart of Religious Education," *Religious Education* 79 (1984), p. 253.
6. Meland, *Fallible Forms and Symbols*, pp. 185-87, draws on Alfred North Whitehead's notion of causal efficacy to speak of the integration and depths of human awareness. Christian teaching seeks to address the full range of perception.
7. Frye, *Great Code*, p. xv.
8. Paulo Freire, *Pedagogy of the Oppressed*, trans. Myra Bergman Ramos (New York: Herder & Herder, 1971), pp. 57-74, rightly argues that a liberative approach to education, in which students learn to reflect critically on the subject matter (and on their lives in the larger context) is superior to a "banking" approach, in which the student only receives and stores data. Christian education needs to be liberative, but in order for it to be liberative, Christians need to have the Christian story in their bank of life, so that they can draw on its resources for critical reflection.
9. On communities of memory, see Robert N. Bellah et al., *Habits of the Heart* (San Francisco: Harper & Row, 1985), pp. 152-55. On the importance of tradition, see Jaroslav Pelikan, *The Vindication of Tradition* (New Haven: Yale University Press, 1974).
10. Mary Elizabeth Moore, *Education for Continuity and Change* (Nashville: Abingdon Press, 1983), p. 109. This image was inspired by the writings of Whitehead.
11. E.g., ibid., pp. 102ff.
12. Charles R. Blaisdell, "Beyond the Profession of Ministry: The Priest, the Teacher, and the Christ," *Encounter* 47 (1986), pp. 50-51.
13. Ibid., p. 51. Here Blaisdell cites Charles R. Foster, *Teaching in the Community of Faith* (Nashville: Abingdon Press, 1982), p. 121.

14. Ibid., pp. 51-52.
15. Thomas C. Oden, *Pastoral Theology: Essentials of Ministry* (San Francisco: Harper & Row, 1983), p. 139, cited in Blaisdell, ibid.
16. Mary C. Boys, "Teaching," p. 264. Boys notes weaknesses in empirical research in learning on pp. 296-97.
17. John McClure, *The Roundtable Pulpit: Collaborative Preaching* (Nashville: Abingdon Press, 1995). For an older statement, see Reuel L. Howe, *Partners in Preaching* (New York: Seabury Press, 1967), pp. 46-48.
18. On the congregation's sense of participation in the sermon, see chap. 4, "Developing the Sermon as an Event of Teaching and Learning."
19. For practical guidance in these matters, see McClure, *The Roundtable Pulpit*.
20. David G. Buttrick, *Homiletic* (Philadelphia: Fortress Press, 1987), pp. 226-27.
21. Ibid. For an example of a preacher from an oldline denomination who is thinking creatively about this ministry, see William Willimon and Stanley Hauerwas, *Preaching to Strangers* (Louisville: Westminster/John Knox Press, 1992), and William Willimon, *The Intrusive Word* (Grand Rapids: Wm. B. Eerdmans, 1994).
22. Fred B. Craddock, *Overhearing the Gospel* (Nashville: Abingdon Press, 1978), p. 108.
23. These litmus tests need to be applied to sermons over a significant period of time. A single sermon cannot always manifest the full range of these concerns. For an exercise designed to chart such concerns, see Ronald J. Allen, *Preaching for Growth* (St. Louis: Chalice Press, 1988), p. 52, and Ronald J. Allen, "The Social Function of Language in Preaching," *Preaching As a Social Act*, ed. Arthur Van Seters (Nashville: Abingdon Press, 1988), p. 183.
24. Richard A. Jensen, *Telling the Story* (Minneapolis: Augsburg Publishing House, 1980), pp. 26-41. In an earlier era, Andrew Blackwood equated the teaching sermon with one that made points in *The Preparation of Sermons* (Nashville: Abingdon/Cokesbury Press, 1948), pp. 140-43.
25. James W. Cox, *Preaching* (San Francisco: Harper & Row, 1985), pp. 11-17.
26. John W. Westerhoff, "The Pastor as Preacher-Teacher," *Homiletic*, vol. 18, no. 2 (1993), pp. 3-4.
27. James Earl Massey, *Designing the Sermon* (Nashville: Abingdon Press, 1980), pp. 61-74.
28. William J. Carl III, *Preaching Christian Doctrine* (Philadelphia: Fortress Press, 1984), pp. 30, 60, 104.
29. H. Grady Davis, *Design for Preaching* (Philadelphia: Fortress Press, 1958), pp. 120-27.
30. Robert Hughes, "Preaching as Lively Teaching?" *Academy Accents*, vol. 5, no. 3 (1989), p. 3.

31. Cox, *Preaching*, p. 12.
32. Thomas G. Long, "When the Preacher Is a Teacher," *Journal for Preachers* vol. 16, no. 2 (1993), p. 24.
33. Ibid.
34. At present, the literature of homiletics has no book in print on the subject of doctrinal preaching. This is a major need.
35. Many of the interpreters of preaching cited in notes 15–32 would be sympathetic to this view, as would Craig Skinner, *The Teaching Ministry of the Pulpit* (Grand Rapids: Baker Book Co., 1973), esp. p. 182.

3. How People Learn from Sermons

1. For a review of "three useful maps of how adults change and develop," see Laurent A. Daloz, *Effective Teaching and Mentoring* (San Francisco: Jossey-Bass, 1986), pp. 43-88.
2. For reviews of different learning styles, see Huey B. Long, *Adult Learning* (Cambridge: Adult Education Co., 1983), pp. 38-120, and S. Messick and Associates, *Individuality in Learning* (San Francisco: Jossey-Bass, 1978).
3. See, for example, Carol Gilligan, *In a Different Voice* (Cambridge: Harvard University Press, 1982), and Mary Field Belenky et al., *Women's Ways of Knowing* (New York: Basic Books, 1986).
4. This chapter draws mainly on principles of adult learning. I do not imply that the preacher ignores children or young people. The pastor can take four factors into account vis-a-vis those groups: (a) Many of the principles articulated in this chapter apply also to the learning patterns of the young; (b) One of the most important ways children and young people learn is simply by being present and a part of what is going on. They learn from the tone and attitude of the service. They frequently pick up rather sophisticated notions from the "adult" sermons, from prayers, hymns, and other experiences. Sometimes they make such associations even when they appear not to pay any attention to the service; (c) The preacher can incorporate materials into the sermon, especially stories, that speak directly to children and young people; (d) Many congregations sponsor a "children's sermon." Among reliable guides for the children's sermon are W. Alan Smith, *Children Belong in Worship* (St. Louis: CBP Press, 1984); David Ng and Virginia Thomas, *Children in the Worshiping Community* (Atlanta: John Knox Press, 1981).
5. Mary C. Boys, "Teaching: The Heart of Religious Education," *Religious Education* 79 (1974), p. 266.
6. For example, see Malcolm S. Knowles, *The Modern Practice of Adult Education*, rev. (Chicago: Association Press, 1980), p. 23.
7. Stephen D. Brookfield, *The Skillful Teacher* (San Francisco: Jossey-Bass, 1990), pp. 163-89.

8. Robert Kegan, *The Evolving Self* (Cambridge: Harvard University Press, 1982), p. 118; Knowles, *Modern Practice*, pp. 77-79.
9. James W. Fowler, *Faith Development and Pastoral Care* (Philadelphia: Fortress Press, 1987), p. 115.
10. Daloz, *Effective Teaching*, p. 237.
11. Bonita L. Benda, *The Silence Is Broken: Preaching on Social Justice Issues* (Th.D. Dissertation, Iliff School of Theology, 1983), pp. 251-52, 274-75; Hans Van der Geest, *Presence in the Pulpit*, trans. Douglas W. Stott (Atlanta: John Knox Press, 1981), pp. 31-68, 143-51.
12. D. Bruce Roberts, "Theological Education and Field Education: A Parallel Process," *Encounter* 54 (1993), p. 288.
13. Knowles, *Modern Practice*, pp. 57-58.
14. Robert M. Smith, *Learning How to Learn* (Cambridge: Adult Education Co., 1982), pp. 106-18. For homiletical application, see the discussion of pre-sermon roundtable learning in John McClure, *The Roundtable Pulpit: Collaborative Preaching* (Nashville: Abingdon Press, 1995).
15. Knowles, *Modern Practice*, p. 163.
16. The situation is quite different in the African American Christian community, where verbal participation in the sermon is frequently encouraged.
17. Shirley J. Farrah, "Lecture," *Adult Learning Methods*, ed. Michael W. Galbraith (Malabar, Fla.: Krieger Publishing Co., 1990), p. 165.
18. Ibid., p. 178.
19. Mark Tennant, "The Psychology of Adult Learning," *Adult Education*, ed. John M. Peters, Peter Jarvis and Associates (San Francisco: Jossey-Bass, 1991), p. 204.
20. Stephen D. Brookfield, *Developing Critical Thinkers* (San Francisco: Jossey-Bass, 1988), pp. 18-23.
21. Ibid., pp. 92-97; Kegan, *Evolving Self*, p. 158.
22. Roberts, "Theological Education," p. 288. My emphasis.
23. For a penetrating study of this phenomenon, see Leon Festinger, Henry W. Riecken, and Stanley Schachter, *When Prophecy Fails* (Minneapolis: University of Minnesota Press, 1956), pp. 25-30.
24. For a helpful work on worldview deconstruction and reconstruction, see Leon McKenzie, *Adult Education and Worldview Construction* (Malabar, Fla.: Krieger Publishing Co., 1991).
25. One of the clearest descriptions of this shift is Darrell Jodock, *The Church's Bible* (Minneapolis: Fortress Press, 1989), esp. pp. 15-24, 51-67.
26. Brookfield, *Developing Critical Thinkers*, p. 93.
27. Ibid., pp. 93-96. For formal interviewing, Brookfield recommends a third criterion—that the interview be conducted in a conversational voice. See further, Ray E. Sanders, "The Art of Questioning," *Adult Learning Methods*, ed. Michael W. Galbraith (Malabar, Fla.: Krieger Publishing Co., 1990), pp. 119-30.

28. Paulo Freire and Antonio Faundez, *Learning to Question*, trans. Tony Coates (Geneva: WCC Publications, 1989), p. 37.
29. Van der Geest, *Presence in the Pulpit*, p. 149.
30. John McClure, "Changes in the Authority, Method, and Message in Presbyterian (UPCUSA) Preaching in the Twentieth Century," *The Confessional Mosaic: Presbyterians and Twentieth Century Theology*, ed. Milton J. Coalter, John M. Mulder, and Louis B. Weeks (Louisville: Westminster/John Knox Press, 1990), p. 280 (n. 96).
31. Roberts, "Theological Education," p. 289. Kegan, *Evolving Self*, pp. 129-32, points out that it is particularly important for learners to be involved in relationships that will remain constant through periods of change. Ideally, the church should provide such constancy.
32. William F. Perry, *Forms of Intellectual and Ethical Development in the College Years* (New York: Holt, Rinehart, and Winston, 1970), pp. 211-13.
33. Tennant, "Psychology of Adult Learning," p. 194.
34. Smith, *Learning How to Learn*, pp. 92-93.
35. Brookfield, *Developing Critical Thinkers*, pp. 89-110.
36. For example, Ephesians 5:21–6:9, Colossians 3:18–4:11; I Peter 2:11–3:12).
37. Brookfield, *Developing Critical Thinkers*, pp. 107-8.
38. For a systems approach to resistance, see Carol Anderson and Susan Stewart, *Mastering Resistance* (New York: Guilford Press, 1983).
39. Brookfield, *Skillful Teacher*, pp. 147-48.
40. Ibid., pp. 149-54.
41. For a perspective on working with issues that inflame the emotions of the congregation, see Ronald J. Allen and William E. Dorman, "Preaching on Emotionally Charged Issues," *Ministry* 1 (Summer 1992), pp. 41-56, as well as Ronald J. Allen, *Preaching the Topical Sermon* (Louisville: Westminster/John Knox Press, 1992), pp. 95-112.
42. Brookfield, *The Skillful Teacher*, pp. 154-62.
43. Ibid., p. 159.
44. Ibid., p. 157.
45. Roger D. Fallot, "When Congregations Won't Listen," *The Christian Ministry* 16 (March 1985), p. 15.
46. Brookfield, *Skillful Teacher*, pp. 160-61. In actual classroom settings, teachers might relieve the total resisters from being required to participate in class activities and give them the freedom to choose what to be involved in. In return, the resisters agree not to be disruptive.
47. On storytelling, see Charles L. Rice, *Interpretation and Imagination* (Philadelphia: Fortress Press, 1970), pp. 66-74, 86-89; Peter M. Morgan, *Storyweaving: Using Stories to Transform Your Congregation* (St. Louis: CBP Press, 1986); Paul Scott Wilson, *Imagination of the Heart: New Understandings in Preaching* (Nashville: Abingdon Press, 1988), pp. 160-67.

48. Two of the most concise discussions of how stories function are Wilson, *Imagination of the Heart*, pp. 143-60, and Mary Elizabeth Moore, "Narrative Teaching: An Organic Methodology," *Process Studies* 17 (1988), pp. 253-57.
49. Susanne K. Langer, *Feeling and Form* (New York: Charles Scribner's Sons, 1953), pp. 208-79.
50. Ibid., p. 24.
51. Daloz, *Effective Teaching*, p. 22.
52. Tennant, "Psychology of Adult Learning," p. 203.
53. Daloz, *Effective Teaching*, p. 229; Brookfield, *Developing Critical Thinkers*, pp. 243, 252.
54. Moore, "Narrative Teaching," p. 257.
55. Brookfield, *Skillful Teacher*, p. 50.
56. One of the most effective approaches in this specific instance may be to tell the biblical story vividly, and perhaps imaginatively elaborate on its details. See Thomas Boomershine, *Story Journey: An Invitation to the Gospel As Storytelling* (Nashville: Abingdon Press, 1988).
57. Raymond J. Wlodkowski, "Strategies to Enhance Adult Motivation to Learn," *Adult Learning Methods*, ed. Galbraith, p. 111.
58. Thomas G. Long, *The Witness of Preaching* (Louisville: Westminster/John Knox Press, 1989), pp. 133-47.
59. David G. Buttrick, *Homiletic: Moves and Structures* (Philadelphia: Fortress Press, 1987), pp. 97-109.
60. Knowles, *Modern Practice*, p. 49; Michael W. Galbraith, "Attributes and Skills of an Adult Educator," *Adult Learning Methods*, pp. 15-16.
61. As an isolated act, awarding a grade is one of the least effective means for evaluating the adult learner.
62. Ideally, of course, evaluation is built into the ministries of the various leadership bodies of the congregation, so that the elders, deacons, program groups, and ministerial staff regularly evaluate the various components of the congregation's life. Evaluation needs to be a part of the church's systemic life.
63. Other forms of receiving feedback include the pastor's conversation with a Pastoral Relations Committee (a small group of laypeople appointed by the congregation to mediate between congregation and pastor) or other official bodies of the church, written survey instruments, or participation in continuing education events in which the pastor's preaching is evaluated.
64. Brookfield, *Developing Critical Thinkers*, p. 232.

4. Developing the Sermon
As an Event of Teaching and Learning

1. For a similar plan of preparation but focused on topical preaching, see Ronald J. Allen, *Preaching the Topical Sermon* (Louisville: Westminster/John Knox Press, 1992), pp. 37-71.

2. Studies in the hermeneutic of suspicion will help preachers become aware of points at which we often are unconsciously controlled or limited by our values, gender, race, ethnic identity, lifestyles and learning styles, and even by the questions we ask. For representative works on the hermeneutic of suspicion, see Paul Ricoeur, *Freud and Philosophy*, trans. Denis Savage (New Haven: Yale University Press, 1970), esp. pp. 20ff.; Elisabeth Schuessler Fiorenza, *Bread Not Stone* (Boston: Beacon Press, 1984), pp. 1-22; Rebecca Chopp, *The Power to Speak* (New York: Crossroad Publishing Co., 1989), pp. 10-39; appropriate passages in *The Hermeneutics Reader*, ed. Kurt Mueller-Vollmer (New York: Continuum Press, 1988). On learning styles, see my chapter 3, note 2.

3. For approaches to assessing needs in the congregation, see Michael W. Galbraith, "Attributes and Skills of an Adult Educator," *Adult Learning Methods*, ed. Michael W. Galbraith (Malabar, Fla.: Krieger Publishing Co., 1990), pp. 8-10.

4. Leander Keck, *The Bible in the Pulpit* (Nashville: Abingdon Press, 1978), pp. 61-64.

5. The preacher should always remember that a lectionary is a servant of the gospel, not the whole of the gospel. For critical evaluation of the strengths and weaknesses of the use of lectionaries as bases for Christian preaching, see Ronald J. Allen, "Preaching and the Christian Year," *Handbook of Contemporary Preaching*, ed. Michael Diduit (Nashville: Broadman Press, 1992), pp. 236-46; Shelly Cochran, *Liturgical Hermeneutics* (Madison, N.J.: Ph. D. Dissertation, Drew University, 1990); Eugene L. Lowry, *Living with the Lectionary* (Nashville: Abingdon Press, 1992); David G. Buttrick, "Preaching the Lectionary: Two Cheers and Some Questions," *Reformed Liturgy and Music*, vol. 28, no. 2 (1994), pp. 77-81; Edward Farley, "Preaching the Bible and Preaching the Gospel," *Theology Today*, vol. 51 (1994), pp. 90-103.

6. The phrase is adapted from Ernest T. Campbell, "Every Battle Isn't Armageddon," *To God Be the Glory*, ed. Theodore A. Gill (Nashville: Abingdon Press, 1973), p. 145.

7. These include becoming aware of the preacher's (and the congregation's) preassociations with the subject.

8. A bibliography of basic resources for preaching on biblical texts is listed in Allen, *Preaching the Topical Sermon*, pp. 146-47.

9. See Charles L. Rice, *Interpretation and Imagination* (Philadelphia: Fortress Press, 1970), pp. 103-9. The best work on the relationship of art and preaching is Charles L. Rice, *The Embodied Word: Preaching as Art and Liturgy*, Fortress Resources on Preaching (Minneapolis: Fortress Press, 1991).

10. Admittedly, the aspects of some aesthetic expressions need to be explained. For instance, paintings from the past often contain details whose significance is lost to the contemporary viewer. The preacher may need to supply information to help the congregation appreciate

the work. But normally, the preacher can describe the piece without clubbing the congregation with the point.

11. Clark M. Williamson, "Preaching the Gospel: Some Theological Reflections," *Encounter* 49 (1988), p. 191.

12. These criteria are discussed more fully in Williamson, "Preaching the Gospel," in Clark M. Williamson and Ronald J. Allen, *A Credible and Timely Word* (St. Louis: Chalice Press, 1991), pp. 71-90, and in Williamson and Allen, *The Teaching Minister* (Louisville: Westminster/John Knox Press, 1991), pp. 65-82.

13. Admittedly, this is the most elusive of the criteria because our understanding of the world changes from time to time, in response to new discoveries and insights.

14. David Watson, *God Does Not Foreclose: The Universal Promise of Salvation* (Nashville: Abingdon Press, 1990) distinguishes between the universal *promise* of salvation and universal salvation itself.

15. In some situations, of course, the congregation is called upon to make an immediate decision or take an immediate action, in the face of uncertain conclusions. In such cases, the community makes the best decision it can, in light of the information it has, trusting in God to make the best of the congregation's decisions and actions. The congregation should acknowledge the relativities of its perspective, remain open for further illumination, and be ever in prayer and study.

16. A clear goal for the learning session is one of the basic principles of adult learning. See Malcolm Knowles, *The Modern Practice of Adult Education* (Chicago: Association Press, 1980), pp. 232-43. On p. 233, Knowles identifies possible outcomes as knowledge (facts, ideas, concepts), reflective thinking (the capacity to interpret data), values and attitudes, sensitivities and feelings, skills.

17. Leading writers in the field of homiletics disagree as to whether this central statement is a hard, clear proposition, or a more general statement that will provide a "soft focus" for the sermon. For the latter, see Eugene Lowry, *How to Preach a Parable* (Nashville: Abingdon Press, 1989), p. 35.

18. I discuss these notions frequently in my writings. I apologize to readers for echoing this material here. However, I consider these concepts to be fundamental to all preaching.

19. For practical methods, see John McClure, *The Roundtable Pulpit: Collaborative Preaching* (Nashville: Abingdon Press, 1995).

5. Five Models for Teaching Sermons

1. Clark M. Williamson and Ronald J. Allen, *The Teaching Minister* (Louisville: Westminster/John Knox Press, 1991), pp. 94, 98-99; Ronald J. Allen, *Preaching the Topical Sermon* (Louisville: Westminster/John Knox Press, 1992), pp. 75-78. See further, Horton Davies, *The Worship*

of the American Puritans, 1629–1730 (New York: Peter Lang, 1990), pp. 77-114, esp. pp. 82-87.

2. Alfred North Whitehead, *The Aims of Education* (New York: The Free Press, 1967, rev. [originally published 1929]), pp. 15, 17-19.

3. There are exceptions to this principle. A person may have a such a direct interest in a subject that she or he immediately initiates a systematic investigation of the subject. For example, corporation A makes widgets. An engineer from corporation A encounters a souped-up widget manufactured by corporation B. The engineer immediately commences an methodical analysis of the super-widget.

4. Whitehead, *Aims of Education*, p. 26.

5. On doctrinal preaching, see William J. Carl, *Preaching Christian Doctrine* (Philadelphia: Fortress Press, 1984), and Allen, *Preaching the Topical Sermon*.

6. For an overview of the history of the interpretation of this phrase, see J. N. D. Kelly, *Early Christian Creeds*, 3rd Ed. (Essex: Longman, 1972), pp. 378-83. There has been considerable discussion as to whether the passage refers to Christ's descent into hell *(ad inferna)* or to Christ's descent among the dead *(ad inferos)*. The tradition generally has preferred the former.

7. Martha Himmelfarb, *Tours of Hell: An Apocalyptic Form in Jewish and Christian Literature* (Philadelphia: Fortress Press, 1985).

8. For a clear outline of the exegetical discussion, see I. Howard Marshall, *I Peter*, IVP New Testament Commentary (Downers Grove, Ill.: InverVarsity Press, 1991), pp. 122-30.

9. These possibilities are reviewed in Kelly, *Early Christian Creeds*, and in Berard L. Marthaler, O.F.M., *The Creed* (Mystic, Conn.: Twenty-Third Publications, 1987), pp. 167-74.

10. Hermann-Josef Lauter, cited in Hans Urs Von Balthasar, *Dare We Hope "That All Men Be Saved"?* trans. David Kipp and Lothar Krauth (San Francisco: Ignatius Press, 1988), p. 213. Emphasis in the original.

11. Cited in Von Balthasar, *Dare We Hope*, p. 214.

12. Isaac Watts, "When I Survey the Wondrous Cross," *The United Methodist Hymnal* (Nashville: The United Methodist Publishing House, 1989), p. 298.

13. This model is inspired by Fred Craddock, *As One Without Authority*, 3rd ed., rev. (Nashville: Abingdon Press, 1979), pp. 124-25, 146.

14. The classical homiletical discussion of the inductive movement in preaching is still Craddock's *As One Without Authority*.

15. Ibid., p. 124.

16. Ibid., p. 146.

17. Ibid., pp. 125-26.

18. See Janet F. Fishburn, *Confronting the Idolatry of the Family: A New Vision of the Household of God* (Nashville: Abingdon Press, 1991).

19. Cliff Kindy, "Barry Yeakle," *Saints and Neighbors: Stories of Church and Community*, ed. Britton W. Johnston and Sally A. Johnson (Chicago: Center for Church and Community Ministries, 1991), p. 130.

20. Ibid.

21. Ibid., pp. 130-31.

22. H. Grady Davis, *Design for Preaching* (Philadelphia: Fortress Press, 1958), p. 154.

23. Ibid.

24. For discussion of preaching on controversial settings, see Allen, *Preaching the Topical Sermon*, pp. 95-112 and Ronald J. Allen and William E. Dorman, "Preaching on Emotionally Charged Issues," *Ministry* vol. 1, no. 1 (1992), pp. 41-56.

25. See further, Ecclesiasticus 1:11-30; 6:18-37; 14:20–15:10, 16:24–17:14; 24:1-34.

26. Some interpreters claim a much closer identification between God and Sophia. For instance, see Elisabeth Schussler Fiorenza, *In Memory of Her* (New York: Crossroad Publishing, 1983), pp. 132-33, and her *Jesus: Miriam's Child, Sophia's Prophet* (New York: Continuum Publishing, 1994). For a comprehensive portrayal of Sophia as an "integrating figure for feminist spirituality," see Susan Cady, Marian Ronan, and Hal Taussig, *Wisdom's Feast* (San Francisco: Harper & Row, 1989).

27. I am indebted to Arthur Vermillion for suggesting this homiletical pattern.

28. On the paradigmatic function of texts from the Old Testament, see John C. Holbert and Ronald J. Allen, *Holy Root, Holy Branches: Christian Preaching from the Old Testament* (Nashville: Abingdon Press, 1995).

29. Donald E. Gowan, *Reclaiming the Old Testament for the Christian Pulpit* (Atlanta: John Knox Press, 1980), p. 198.

30. Jessie Brown Pounds, *Memorial Selections* (Chicago: Disciples Publication Society, 1921), p. 52.

31. For the idea of using Ricoeur's approach as a model for the sermon, I am indebted to Ted Peters, "Hermeneutics and Homiletics," *Dialog* 21 (1982), pp. 121-29. I give the idea a slightly different spin. Ricoeur's writing is sometimes thick and hard to penetrate. One of the most lucid expositions is Rebecca Button Prichard, "Conflict, Suspicion, and Accommodation," *Encounter* 55 (1994), pp. 221-36. I offer a less technical overview in my *Contemporary Biblical Interpretation for Preaching* (Valley Forge: Judson Press, 1984), pp. 131-34.

32. See, for example, Paul Ricoeur, *Freud and Philosophy: An Essay in Interpretation*, trans. Denis Savage (New Haven: Yale University Press, 1970), pp. 20ff.

33. In this part of the sermon, I follow Samuel Terrien, *The Psalms and Their Meaning for Today* (Indianapolis: Bobbs-Merrill, 1952), pp. 228-38. For a more recent review of scholarly discussion, see Peter

C. Craigie, *Psalms 1–50*, Word Biblical Commentary (Waco: Word Books, 1983), pp. 203-9; Artur Weiser, *The Psalms*, trans. Herbert Hartinell (Philadelphia: The Westminster Press, 1962), pp. 145-49; Patrick D. Miller, Jr., *Interpreting the Psalms* (Philadelphia: Fortress Press, 1986), pp. 112-19.
34. These characteristics are derived from a summer when I lived on a farm which kept sheep, and are confirmed in *Encyclopedia Americana*.

6. Plans for Systematic Teaching from the Pulpit

1. The Consultation on Common Texts, *The Revised Common Lectionary* (Nashville: Abingdon Press, 1992).
2. The biblical readings in the first segment of Ordinary Time (the Sundays after Epiphany) continue the emphases of Epiphany and are chosen on the basis of *lectio selecta*.
3. For history and discussion, see Hoyt L. Hickman et al., *The New Handbook of the Christian Year* (Nashville: Abingdon Press, 1992).
4. For the patterns of these relationships, see *The Revised Common Lectionary*, pp. 12-18.
5. Note that the readings from the Hebrew Bible can relate to the Gospel in one of three modes: parallel content, contrasting content, content that is fulfilled in the New Testament (see *The Revised Common Lectionary*, pp. 12-13). See further John C. Holbert and Ronald J. Allen, *Holy Root, Holy Branches: Christian Preaching from the Old Testament* (Nashville: Abingdon Press, 1995), chap. 6.
6. In still broader perspective, of course, the pastor preaches neither the text nor the theme of the season or day. Ultimately, the preacher preaches the Gospel, using text, season, or day only as a point of entry.
7. For overviews of discussion on positive and negative qualities of lectionary preaching, see the sources in note 5, chapter 4.
8. I base this observation on many years of experience of leading Bible study series in many congregations of the oldline denominations. Attendance usually holds high for the first month, but begins to wane by the end of the second month.
9. This notion is developed further in Ronald J. Allen, "Preaching on a Theme from the Bible," *Pulpit Digest* vol. 75, no. 526 (1994), pp. 78-86.
10. The term *theme* is not a technical category of biblical scholarship. It refers loosely to ideas, images, and realities that are similar in concern and motif, and are found in different parts of the Bible.
11. Edward Farley, "Preaching the Bible and Preaching the Gospel," *Theology Today* 51 (1994), pp. 90-103.
12. For examples of other themes that can form bases for series of sermons, see Norbert Lohfink, S. J., *Great Themes from the Old Testament*, trans. Ronald Walls (Edinburgh: T & T Clark, 1982), and John C. Holbert and Ronald J. Allen, *Holy Root, Holy Branches: Christian Preaching from the Old Testament*, chap. 4. Many of the volumes in the series

Overtures to Biblical Scholarship (published by Fortress Press) have a thematic quality. For example, see Claus Westermann, *Blessing in the Bible and in the Life of the Church*, trans. Keith Crim (Philadelphia: Fortress Press, 1978); Sharon Ringe, *Jesus, Liberation, and the Biblical Jubilee* (Philadelphia: Fortress Press, 1985); Samuel E. Balentine, *Prayer in the Hebrew Bible* (Minneapolis: Fortress Press, 1993).

13. Thomas G. Long, "When the Preacher Is a Teacher," *Journal for Preachers* vol. 16, no. 2 (1993), p. 26.

14. For practical development of these strategies, see chap. 4.

15. Richard W. Jensen is co-pastor of Third Christian Church, Indianapolis, Indiana.

16. The survey was taken by The Reverend Martha Grace Reese at Carmel Christian Church, Carmel, Indiana.

7. Teaching a Core Curriculum from the Pulpit

1. Lyman Lundeen, "The Authority of the Word in Process Perspective," *Encounter* 36 (1975), p. 281.

2. For a survey of the different ways in which Christians regard the authority of the Bible today, see *Conservative, Liberal, Moderate*, ed. Charles R. Blaisdell (St. Louis: CBP Press, 1991).

3. The terms *right* and *left* are unfortunate. They are taken from the political arena and have the tendency to polarize their users. I use them for convenience. But I do so with regret.

4. Churches on the right also make use of experience, tradition, and reason. To wit: The Bible generally assumes the validity of slavery, yet no Christian communion known to me in North America recognizes slavery as an acceptable form of human relationship.

5. Edward Farley, *Ecclesial Reflection* (Philadelphia: Fortress Press, 1982), pp. 165-70.

6. Uncertainties regarding authority in the contemporary world arise, in part, because of the shift from modern consciousness (in which science was the reigning authority) to postmodern consciousness (in which bases of authority are more diffuse). Among the clearest descriptions of postmodernism (and its relationship to premodernism and modernism) are Darrell Jodock, *The Church's Bible* (Minneapolis: Fortress Press, 1989), pp. 15-18; James B. Miller, "The Emerging Postmodern World," *Postmodern Theology*, ed. Frederic B. Burnham (San Francisco: Harper & Row Publishers, 1989), pp. 1-19. On different types of postmodern thought, see esp. the State University of New York Press Series in Constructive Postmodern Theology, ed. David R. Griffin. Note especially *Varieties of Postmodern Theology*, ed. David Ray Griffin, William A. Beardlee, and Joe Holland (Albany: State University of New York Press, 1989).

7. Preachers often lament the biblical illiteracy of the church, but we could lament even more the theological illiteracy of today's people.

8. In chap. 4, I noted a convenient way for the preacher to get in touch with the tradition in specific points by referring to the standard dictionaries of church history and theology.
9. See particularly Paul Ricoeur, *The Conflict of Interpretations: Essays in Hermeneutics,* ed. Don Ihde (Evanston: Northwestern University Press, 1974). For an update, see David Tracy, "Hermeneutical Reflections in the New Paradigm," *Paradigm Change in Theology,* ed. Hans Kueng and David Tracy, trans. Margaret Koehl (Edinburgh: T & T Clark, 1989), pp. 34-62.
10. Alfred North Whitehead, *Process and Reality,* Rev. Ed., ed. David R. Griffin and Donald W. Sherburne (New York: The Free Press, 1979), p. 15.
11. Clark M. Williamson, "Preaching the Gospel: Some Theological Reflections," *Encounter* 49 (1988), p. 191.
12. Two of the best discussions of these phenomena are Leander Keck, *The Bible in the Pulpit* (Nashville: Abingdon Press, 1978), pp. 100-104; D. Newell Williams, "Disciples Piety: A Historical Review with Implications for Spiritual Formation," *Encounter* 47 (1986), pp. 13-17.
13. In the worst instances, the preacher can drift from moralism into works righteousness.
14. Compatibility with the contemporary worldview is an elusive criterion. The contemporary worldview changes from time to time, in response to fresh data and angles of vision.
15. For literature exploring the changes in church and culture, see chap. 1, note 19.
16. Joe R. Jones, "On Doing Church Theology Today," *Encounter* 40 (1979), pp. 279-80.
17. An extremely helpful guide to the larger theological conversation within which the discussion of the purpose of the church takes place is William C. Placher, *Unapologetic Theology: A Christian Voice in a Pluralistic Conversation* (Louisville: Westminster/John Knox Press, 1989).
18. As is often the case, Willimon and Hauerwas have more mature and inclusive views than many who represent them.
19. Stanley Hauerwas and William Willimon, *Resident Aliens: Life in the Christian Colony* (Nashville: Abingdon Press, 1989).
20. For example, see David Tracy, *The Analogical Imagination* (New York: Crossroad Publishing, 1981), pp. 3-46; Tracy, with John B. Cobb, Jr., *Talking About God: Doing Theology in the Context of Modern Pluralism* (New York: The Seabury Press, 1981), pp. 1-16.
21. In this context, justice refers to the enactment of love in all relationships, so that all people and communities live in security, mutuality, and support.
22. David G. Buttrick, *Homiletic: Moves and Structures* (Philadelphia: Fortress Press, 1987), pp. 420-24.

23. Joseph E. Faulkner, "What Are They Saying? A Content Analysis of 206 Sermons Preached in the Christian Church (Disciples of Christ) During 1988," *A Case Study of Mainstream Protestantism*, ed. D. Newell Williams (Grand Rapids: Wm. B. Eerdmans/St. Louis: Chalice Press, 1991), p. 423.

Appendix

1. This worksheet is based on chapter 4.
2. These styles and qualities are identified in chapter 3.

INDEX